Cool Cardboard Instruments

to make & play

Dennis Waring

Sterling Publishing Co., Inc. New York

A Sterling/Tamos Book

A Sterling/Tamos Book
© 2000 Dennis G. Waring

Sterling Publishing Co., Inc.
387 Park Avenue South
New York, NY 10016-8810

Tamos Books Inc.
300 Wales Avenue
Winnipeg, MB Canada R2M 2S9

10 9 8 7 6 5 4 3 2 1

Distributed in Canada by Sterling Publishing Co., Inc.
c/o Canadian Manda Group, One Atlantic Avenue, Suite 105
Toronto, Ontario, Canada M6K 3E7
Distributed in Great Britain and Europe by Chris Lloyd,
463 Ashley Road, Parkstone, Poole, Dorset, BH14 OAX, England
Distributed in Australia by Capricorn Link (Australia) Pty Ltd.
P.O. Box 6651, Baulkham Hills, Business Centre, NSW 2153 Australia

Design   A. O. Osen
Photography   Dennis G. Waring
Illustrations   Leo Simoens

Printed in Hong Kong

Canadian Cataloging-in-Publication Data
Waring, Dennis, G. 1945–
     Cool cardboard instruments to make & play
     "A Sterling/Tamos book."
     Includes index.
     ISBN 1-895569-62-1

1. Musical instruments--Construction--Juvenile literature.
2. Paperboard. I. Title.

ML460.W275 2000   j784.192'3   C00-920098-3

Library of Congress Cataloging-in-Publication Data
Waring, Dennis, 1945–
     Cool cardboard instruments to make & play / Dennis Waring.
        p. cm.
     "A Sterling/Tamos book."
     Includes index.
     ISBN 1-895569-62-1
        1. Musical instruments--Construction. I. Title.

     ML460 .W278 2000
     784.192'3--dc21   00-030816

Tamos Books Inc. acknowledges the financial support of the Government of
Canada through the Book Publishing Development Program (BPIDP) for our
publishing activities.

NOTE If you prefer to work in metric measurements, to convert
inches to millimeters multiply by 25.4.

ISBN 1-895569-62-1

About the Author   Dr. Dennis G. Waring is an
ethnomusicologist, educator, instrument maker,
collector, performer, and arts consultant who
teaches World Music, American Music, and Music
Education courses on the university level, and is
involved in public education in primary, middle,
and high schools. He travels and lectures
throughout North America and journeys around
the world to gather new instruments and ideas.

My thanks and appreciation to
David Magnuson, my assistant, the creator of many
projects and ideas, and without whose help this
book would never have been realized. Also, David
Cross of Backyard Music for encouraging the idea
of making instruments from cardboard, Michael
Nielsen, designer for the Stone Container
Corporation, for professional insight into how
factories process corrugated cardboard, to Kristen
Fortier for helping decorate the instruments, and all
the children and adults who participated in playing
the instruments and posing for photographs: Maya
and Drew Keleher; Tony, Teddy, Simon, and Wendy
Mason-Sherwood; Mia Falco; Steve Lefebvre; David,
Sarah, Karl, and Jason Magnuson; Kristin Fortier;
Randy, Emma Weiss, Giovanni Ciarlo, and Michael
Fraser.

Contents

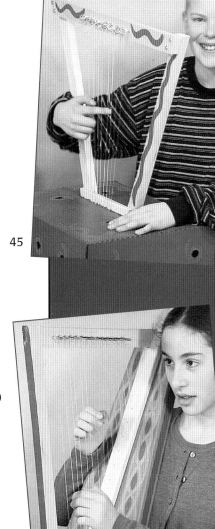

Introduction

Making a cardboard musical instrument can be as easy as putting a stick through a box and attaching a couple of nylon fishing line strings. Easier yet, use the box as a simple drum. Such simple music-makers produce a pleasing enough tone and can be used for hours of fun. There are, however, many ways to exploit cardboard and wood to greatly enhance the final outcome of the instrument-making project; the amazing tonal quality that can be achieved is quite remarkable.

At first it may be difficult to imagine that something as refined as a musical instrument can be made from corrugated cardboard.

However, cardboard is one of the easiest materials to cut, fold, and glue, it is nonharmful and recyclable, it is easy to find, and it is a resonant material, which is a prerequisite for producing good sound. Although musical instruments work on a wide variety of complex technical principles (i.e. physics), cardboard can accommodate most all scientific necessities. When combined with wood for the tension-bearing elements—those parts that hold the strings—a cardboard instrument will amaze and delight the player.

Cardboard comes in a huge variety of types: number of corrugations per inch, style of facing, single and double thicknesses, even plastic "cardboard." "Whatever-you-find" varieties of cardboard can be tried and discarded if they do not produce an acceptable sound.

The kinds of wood needed to reinforce some designs can

be found in local home supply centers, lumberyards, or hardware stores. Common wood products such as lattice, furring, doweling, wood trim, and other premachined woods minimize the need for milling larger pieces. Start a collection of throw-away wood scraps that can be used for braces, bridges, and other small components.

The projects in this book range from using ordinary

cardboard boxes and attaching sticks and strings in an appropriate configuration to designing and constructing instruments from scratch. The ideas presented here give precise instructions for making each project, but they also serve as inspiration for experiments for your own musical creations. Use your imagination. Not every experiment may work but you will learn from experience.

The majority of projects are stringed instruments simply because cardboard accommodates that medium more than for wind or percussion instruments. Wind instruments produce a moisture problem and cardboard percussion instruments generally do not last very long. Nevertheless, a few suggestions are included for these instruments.

Part 1 emphasizes using found or stock materials for instruments such as cardboard boxes, 1x2s, 2x4s, and other scrap wood, and fishing line of heavier gauges. Often the shape and size of the box itself suggest an instrument. After you make your first instrument, you will never again look at a cardboard box in the same way. A free imagination, utility

Top *Samisen (Asian long-neck lute), Koto (Asian zither)*
Middle *African tube zither*
Bottom *Greek lyre*

knife, and lots of duct tape could make an heirloom from a pizza box!

Part 2 demonstrates how to design a sound box pattern that works, and how to cut, fold, and glue your own creations. Once you master the basic principles of box–making, there is no end to the design possibilities. Some woodworking experience is helpful but most projects here can be made from

simple wood pieces using basic hand tools or common electric tools. The combination of cardboard and wood produces excellent working instruments that are easy to make and fun to play. In fact, working with a material as informal as cardboard has great advantages.

One can experiment and create with virtually no expenditure or prior experience. With cardboard, risks are minimal and there are no such things as mistakes.

As this project developed, my quest for design inspirations came from my academic studies in ethnomusicology. In this instance, however, I have not taken an academic approach but rather one which embraces large doses of imagination and humor. Therefore, any instrument with a triangular sound box becomes a "Russian balalaika," mounting multiple strings on an elongated box makes a "Japanese koto," and so forth. Although I have taken great license in this

regard, I trust readers will join in with the spirit of fun and use ideas from around the world for their own creations. It is a good way to learn about different cultures and their music.

Tools and Materials

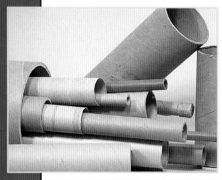

Boxes and tubes   Cardboard boxes are everywhere. Naturally, a more substantial box will stand up better over time and use, but almost any kind of cardboard box will work for the musical instruments in this book. Experiment with size and shape and learn and refine as you go. Some projects suggested in this book utilize cardboard tubing as well as boxes. Inquire at your local home center store for different grades and thicknesses of material. Choose carpet tubing, mailing and packing tubes, poster tubes, tubes used as forms for concrete pilings and pillars, and tubes from household products. They all come in varying diameters and wall thicknesses and all will be useful.

Cutting tools   Perhaps the most important tool used to fashion cardboard is a utility knife appropriate for the purpose. It is inexpensive, available at any hardware store or home center, and useful for many other cutting applications as well. Its ample handle and relatively short blade (easily replaced when dull), makes it exceptionally safe. Some feature a retractable blade. X-acto knives and extra heavy-duty scissors are also useful for cutting and trimming.

Rulers   A quality metal 12 in ruler and a yardstick are necessary for drawing and cutting straight edges. A tape measure is also useful.

Worktable   A standard woodworking bench or sturdy folding table with a protective cover (scrap sheet of plywood, cardboard, or formica) works well.

Wood   All the wood pieces necessary to make these instruments are available at local home centers and lumberyards. Softwoods such as pine and spruce are easier to use for simple instruments, while hardwoods such as maple and mahogany can withstand the greater string tension for complex instruments. Generally 1x2 in material is a good basic stock for stringed instrument necks and frameworks. Build up your collection of various sizes of wood scraps; otherwise, try to use standard wood sizes as they come from the store to minimize milling and sawing rough stock. Thin plywood (⅛ in) is also suggested for the soundboards of the more complex instruments for long-term service.

Basic woodworking tools   A small hammer, screwdriver, awl, drill, appropriate hand saw, and file and sandpaper for working the wood are all that is necessary for getting started. Power tools are not necessary, but if you have them they facilitate various steps in preparing the wood components on some of the more complex instruments. The projects in this book can all be made using hand tools only, but a drill press and jigsaw, for example, make for less work.

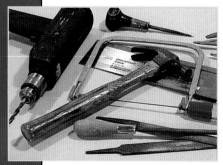

Adhesives   Several different bonding agents may be considered to join together the various pieces of each project. Duct tape and packing tape are the easiest way to make a box. Different colors of tape can be used for a more decorative touch. Heavy staples may also be useful. Hot glue applied with a glue gun applicator is an excellent way to bond cardboard parts and some wood parts. Its short drying time allows for components to be hand held in place. Gluing cardboard and wood with a standard white glue or yellow glue is more professional but some clamping of parts is required because of the longer drying time. Wood glue should be used on parts that need extra structural stability. Rubber cement or contact cement will work on cardboard as well, but because

of its toxic nature, it is not always the best choice. Each gluing agent has its own requirements. Be sure to follow the manufacturer's directions. Joining pieces of wood may also be done by using nails, screws, staples, or tacks for quick construction. Using more advanced woodworking techniques employing complex wood joinery, wood glue, and clamps may appeal to the more accomplished crafter.

Sealing and finishing   An enormous variety of finishing products work well with cardboard, although non-penetrating finishes are best. Sealing the cardboard is important for wind instruments to keep moisture in check. A base coat of the color of your choice provides a good foundation for more decorative detail. Depending on the project, it may be advisable to paint or finish parts of the instrument before it is completely assembled. Acrylics, latex, varnishes, or high-tech varieties of finishes are recommended. Use exterior rather than penetrating finishes. Never use oils on cardboard.

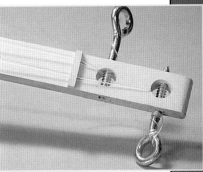

Decorating   Possibilities for instrument decoration are endless. Tasteful ornamenting will remove the industrial look of the cardboard. Use purchased stencils and stickers, colored magic markers, pen and inks of different colors, or posterboard paints or crayons. Visit your local art store outlet for other options. For ethnically inspired instruments, use motifs and symbols appropriate to that culture. Draw the designs yourself, trace them, or ask an artist friend to help.

Tuning mechanisms and hitch pins

Screw eyes   Various dimensions of wood screws with different size eyelets on top are the easiest and quickest mechanisms for tensioning strings. They hold the string tension very well. No. 10 size is good for general purpose tuners. Nylon strings are easier to use than metal strings because strings need to be tied to the screw eye. (Don't forget to pass the string through the eye so that the string will tension as the screw is screwed into the wood.) Friction tuning pegs (violin style), zither pins (autoharp style), and machine tuning mechanisms (guitar style) may be used for more complex instruments. To secure the tail end of the string requires hitch pins (small sizes of nails, tacks, brads, or pre-drilled holes will work for this purpose).

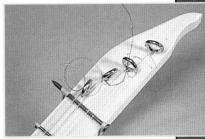

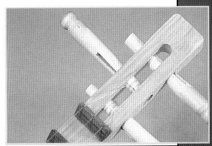

Nylon fishing line makes excellent strings. *Above Bridges on an African tube zither*

Strings

Use various gauges of ordinary monofilament nylon fishing line for less complex instruments. Fishing line comes in a wide spectrum of gauges or weights, (measured in lbs). A forty-, fifty-, or sixty-pound test line is a good place to start. For large, low sounding instruments, use thicker string. Nylon weed trimmer line comes in several thick gauges (some too thick for musical application) and can be used on the bass range of multi-stringed instruments such as the harp or lyre and for the inherently low-sounding strings on projects such as the string bass. Highly processed music wire (steel, brass, or bronze) made specifically for musical instruments is also readily available.

Be sure to reinforce all parts of the instrument to deal with the extra tension. Music wire comes in plain and wound varieties measured to the thousandths of an inch. Wound strings have a binding around a core string which allows for a lower range than plain strings. The thinner strings used on commercial guitars and banjos are generally the most useful. Rolls of custom gauge wire manufactured for instruments such as harpsichords and hammered dulcimers are also available for more ambitious projects.

Tuning

String material, number of strings, thickness of strings, string lengths, string tension, are all variables that determine the final sound of an instrument. The instructions in this book provide some general guidelines and suggestions to help you get your instrument up and running; however, tuning the various instruments will depend on you.

The general rule is that the tighter the string, the clearer the pitch. Using the first string as an indicator, select and attach other strings. Musically, strings tuned in unisons and octaves are very strong. Intervals of fourths and fifths are also basic to most stringed instruments. Use a standard musical instrument or electronic tuner to help, or ask a musician to show you how. Careful tuning takes patience and is crucial for getting the best results from the instrument.

Fretting

Fret placement is important if you expect to play real music. In many cases, marks drawn on the fingerboard are all that is necessary. Otherwise, use big staples or tied-on nails. For fret placement on simple instruments, rely on your musical sense as to where they should go. A piano, harmonica, pitch pipe, or other pitched instrument may help. Or use small electronic tuners to tune strings and determine fret placements. There is even computer software available to quickly calculate fret placements for any string length.

Bridge Most stringed instruments of the lute family require a bridge and nut which hold the strings above the fingerboard and sound box and delineate a "string length" which is necessary for placement of frets. Zithers often require multiple bridges. Details are given with each project.

Nut Small piece of wood that is notched to help align the strings.

Peg head This piece of wood holds the screw eyes or tuning mechanisms to anchor strings.

Frets on an East Indian tube-neck lute (sitar)

Part 1 Simple Versions of Instruments

Stringed Instruments (Chordophones)

Early instrument makers found that a stick can be poked through a box-like container in any number of ways. The primary consideration is that the intended trajectory of the attached strings be free of obstruction in order to vibrate freely. To help accomplish this, one or more bridges are positioned to lift the strings from the top of the sound box. The height of the bridge (and an optional nut at the tuner end) determines the ease of playing. Adjusting the closeness of the strings to the fingerboard is called setting the string action.

Other instruments such as simple harps and lyres require connecting two or more pieces of wood for an appropriate framework configuration. Wood components can be fastened together in several ways: nails, screws, and glue are standard.

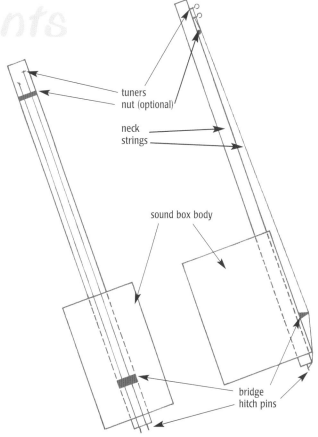

tuners
nut (optional)

neck
strings

sound box body

bridge
hitch pins

Simple Guitars and Lutes

The easiest and most common homemade stringed instruments belong to the lute and guitar family: instruments with a neck that protrudes from a smaller sound box. In most cases the size of the neck and box should be proportional although almost any shape or size of box will work and the neck can be almost any length you wish. Use packing boxes, pizza boxes, shoe boxes, egg cartons, oatmeal and salt containers, cereal boxes, or modify boxes to meet your own specifications.

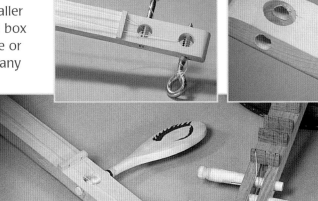

For simple tuning devices use screw eyes of various sizes placed in contrasting configurations or old-fashioned clothespins and tapered wood dowels of varying diameters.

One-String Strummer

Materials

egg carton, oatmeal box, or other small container,
    or 2 heavy duty paper picnic plates glued
    together for sound box body
broomstick or other wood stick for neck
wood piece for bridge
nylon fishing line
nail and screw eye for hitch pin and tuner

Procedure

1 Measure and cut holes through container to accommodate the chosen stick for the neck. Position stick close to the playing surface of the container for easy fingering.

2 Hammer a small nail in the tail end of instrument and screw eye tuner into the other end.

3 Tie double knots in string to secure to the nail and screw eye tuner. Pass the string through the eye so that the string will tension as the screw is screwed into the wood. Tighten string.

4 Place a small piece of wood or dowel between the strings and the box to act as a bridge. Tune to desired pitch and strum away. Make a simple plastic pick, if desired.

Any carton, box, or small container will work as a sound box. Two heavy-duty paper picnic plates glued together will also work.

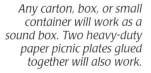

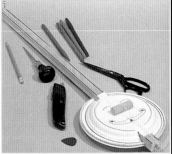

Simple Box Guitar

Materials

small- to medium-size box for sound
    box body
appropriate-size stick for neck
piece of wood for bridge
screw eyes for tuners
nylon string
small nails for hitch pins

Procedure

1 Choose one face of the box to be
the soundboard. Carefully measure
and cut matching holes through the
box, as shown, so that the stick (neck
of instrument) spikes completely
through and comes close to or
touches the inside of the box face for
extra stability. The stick should fit
snugly. Insert stick, as shown.

Left *One-string strummer*   Right *Simple box guitar*

2 Decide on how many strings to put on the guitar.
There should be enough space between strings and
tuners so they don't interfere with each other. Generally,
two or three strings spaced ½ in apart will suffice for
these projects.

3 Hammer small nails (hitch pins) for anchoring the
strings at the tail end of the neck. Plot the placement of
the screw eyes at the head of the instrument. Do not
screw the tuner in too far until after the strings are
attached.

4 Secure strings from nails to screws. Place a bridge under
all the strings. Shallow grooves may be sawn or filed into
the bridge to keep the strings from slipping around. Tighten
the string by turning the screw into the wood.

5 Tune strings in unison, octaves, fifths, or fourths to use
standard approaches to playing, or simply tune strings to
your own personal liking and play away. Experiment with
other boxes.

Marking neck placement

Cutting neck hole

Fitting neck to box

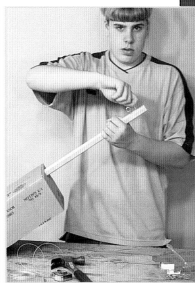

*Attaching screw eye tuners
and string*

Pizza Box Guitar

Materials

any size pizza box for sound box body
appropriate length of stick for neck
piece of wood for bridge
screw eyes for tuners
nylon string
small screw eyes or nails for hitch pins

Procedure

1 Buy a takeout pizza and save the box. Some boxes work better than others. The sturdier the box, the better.

2 Find a stick as long or short as you wish (within reason).

3 Cut holes or flaps in the box edge or corner and insert the stick.

4 For stringing, start screw eyes at one end of the stick and small hitch pins at the other.

5 Tie strings to hitch pins and secure to screw eyes. Begin to tighten strings.

6 Slide bridge under string and experiment with placement to find the best sound.

7 Tune strings to desired pitches. Strings should be relatively tight for the best sound.

8 Strum away.

Width of neck and where hole is placed to receive neck are variable.

Cutting hole for neck

Bridge/tailpiece configuration

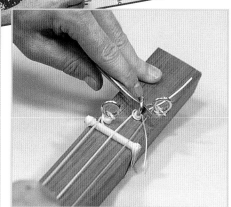

Tuning strings using a lever

Middle East Lute

The Middle East lute, called the oud (or ud), is the likely ancestor to the European Renaissance lute and Spanish guitar. Lutes are typically characterized by a large curved-back sound box constructed of many slats or staves of wood carefully glued together, and a relatively short neck with various numbers of strings. To simulate the bowl shape usual to this family of lutes the cardboard box is truncated.

Materials

medium-size box for sound box body
appropriate-size stick for neck
small wood pieces for nut and bridge
screw eyes for tuners
nylon string
small nails for hitch pins

Procedure

1 Cut the box flaps so they come together, as shown. Duct tape the seams, as shown.

2 For this style of instrument, choose a relatively short wide piece of wood for the neck. Determine width of the neck by the number of strings desired.

3 For variety, the peg head can be cut, as shown, so the screw eye tuners function from the sides rather than the top of the peg head. This configuration requires a nut to help align the strings for playing. Saw slots or drill small equidistant guide holes through the bridge, as shown.

4 Measure, mark, and cut holes into the box to receive the neck. Insert neck and hammer nails in the tail end for hitch pins. Attach screw eyes to the peg head.

5 Slightly thicker strings tuned somewhat loosely will give a lower, more characteristic sound, but you may have to experiment with various gauges to get the right combination.

6 Secure strings to hitch pins, thread through the nut and attach to screw eyes so that strings tighten as the screw is turned.

7 Slide bridge between the strings and sound box top and position where it sounds best. Tune in unisons, fifths, and octaves.

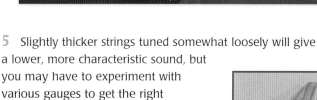

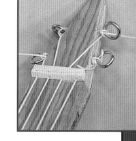

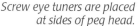

Screw eye tuners are placed at sides of peg head.

Cutting box to a more "bowl-shaped" configuration

13

Chinese Moon Guitar

With its large, round, thinly-sliced resonator and very short neck, the Chinese moon guitar, called the yueqin, is one of the most picturesque instruments in the world. Because of the expanse of the soundboard, a small foundation "saddle" of wood glued between the top and bridge of the instrument will help distribute the pull of the strings across the soundboard.

Materials

larger diameter construction tubing and
    2-ply cardboard for sound box body
appropriate-size stick for neck
old-style round clothespins or slit dowels for tuners
small wood pieces for nut and frets
bridge assemblage
nylon string

Procedure

1 Cut a 2 in thick slice of 12 in (or larger) construction tube for the body framework.

2 Select appropriate stick of wood for the neck and cut opposing notches into the cardboard tube to receive the neck, as shown.

3 Measure and mark the peg head where a slot will be. Use old-fashioned clothespins, whittled and sanded to fit a slightly smaller hole, as tuners. The split in the clothespin causes it to compress in the hole and thus hold the string tension. Or use wood doweling with a slit-like cut.

4 Cut the peg head slot with a coping saw or jigsaw. File uniform. Drill holes in side of peg head to receive chosen tuners, as shown.

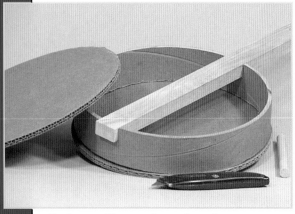

Neck, sound box, and soundboard

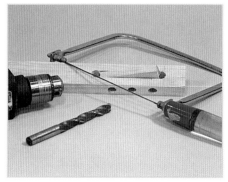

Preparing peg head

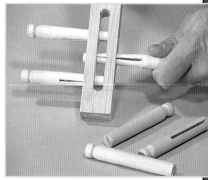

Fitting tuners

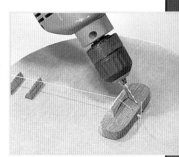

Drilling holes in saddle for securing strings

5 From flat 2-ply cardboard, cut the soundboard and back of the moon guitar using the tube as a pattern. (If tube is large in diameter glue a brace or strut to the inside of the top for reinforcement.)

6 Glue components together using hot glue or wood glue. Glue neck to body. Glue top and back to body.

7 The bridge arrangement here is a saddle footing glued to the soundboard with the actual bridge sitting on top. In this style of bridge, the strings attach directly to and pull on the bridge instead of pushing down on the bridge as in previous projects. Drill holes in the saddle, as shown. Glue the saddle to the soundboard securely. Do not glue bridge to saddle at this time.

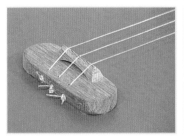
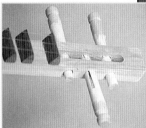

8 Since this project has tall wood frets, the relative height of nut, bridge, and frets should be thought about carefully. Make nut and frets so that the nut height is slightly more than fret heights. Then make and adjust the bridge height so that the strings pass near to the tops of the frets without touching. Tie knots in the end of the strings, thread strings though saddle, over bridge, and secure to tuning pegs.

9 Once everything is finally adjusted, glue nut and bridge in place.

10 Bring one string up to desired pitch and slide each fret into place until desired scale is achieved. A five-note, pentatonic scale (1−2−3−5−6 scale degrees) is common to these instruments. Glue frets into place.

11 Hold as a guitar and strum briskly.

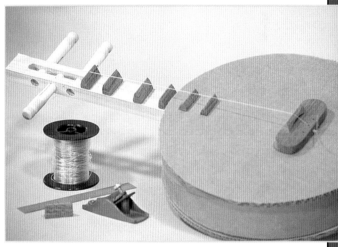

Saddle is glued to soundboard, bridge sits on top to hold strings. Bridge and nut should be higher than frets.

Clothespin or dowel tuners should be fitted carefully so they will hold string tension.

Asian Long-Neck Lute

The Asian long-neck lute (samisen) is common in East Asia. This family of lutes have small sound boxes and long thin necks. The extra string length allows for a greater range and more possible notes.

Procedure

1 Use an 8 in cardboard tube and cut a 3 in section.
2 Select a relatively long 1½ in x ½ in stick for the neck. Cut notches in the tube to receive the neck, as shown.
3 Prepare the peg head, as shown. Drill two large holes in the face of the peg head to receive strings and smaller holes on the side of the peg head for tuners. In this instance, holes and tuners are shaped so that tuners friction fit the holes (drill holes slightly smaller than the diameter of the tuning pegs). If using wood, sand the tuners to a slight taper so they fit snugly into the hole. Drill tiny holes into the tuner for attaching string. Use wood dowels, large screw eyes, or even wood mixing spoons for tuners, as shown.
4 Cut a soundboard from 2-ply cardboard using the tube itself as a template. Glue neck to tube and soundboard top to body.
5 Hammer small nails to tail end of instrument for hitch pins.
6 If you use a cardboard top, make a bridge assemblage, as shown, by cutting a small platform for the bridge so the bridge itself will not dent the top.
7 Small holes or shallow grooves in the nut help guide the strings along the proper trajectory to the bridge.
8 Use strings of the same gauge tuned to the same unison pitch. Medium tension will give the most characteristic sound.

Left *Samisen*   Right *Koto (p 64)*

Materials

cardboard construction tube and
    2-ply cardboard for sound box body
appropriate-size stick for neck
small wood pieces for nut and bridge
tuners and hitch pins
nylon string

Below *Optional screw eye tuners*
Right *Bridge placement*
Bottom left *Mixing spoon tuners*
Bottom right *Bridge on platform*

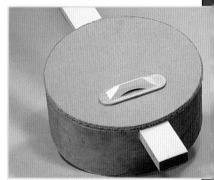

Neck, sound box tube, and soundboard

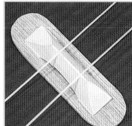

East Indian Tube-Neck Lute

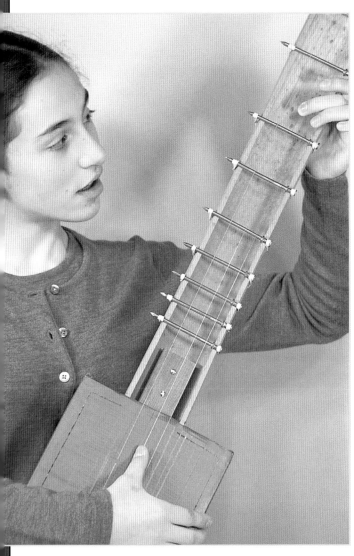

Materials

cardboard box for sound box body
cardboard tube for neck
strip of wood for neck reinforcement
piece of wood for bridge
screw eyes for tuners
metal music wire
long nails for frets
rubber bands

Procedure

1 Find an appropriate size box for sound box.
2 Cut approximately 20 in of 3 in diameter cardboard tube lengthwise with a sharp saw. Sand surface smooth.
3 Cut a length of wood so that after it is spiked through the box, it protrudes about 3 in on the neck side and 1 in on the tail side.
4 Screw and bolt the wood reinforcer to the tube, as shown.
5 Attach screw eyes to tail end of instrument for tuning.
6 Drill holes into the head end of the tube neck for securing strings (a bolt is used to reinforce the tube at this end).
7 Attach nail frets with rubber bands. The first nail at the head end acts as the nut (see photograph). Once fixed, frets may be slid into any scale configuration, one of the main features of these instruments.
8 Mount strings, as shown. Begin to tighten strings. Insert bridge on the soundboard. Cut shallow grooves in bridge to help seat the strings. Make any necessary adjustments.
9 Traditionally, this instrument's music is strictly melodic with strong drones. For this effect, tune strings to unison, octaves, fifths, and fourths. Play along one melody string and let the others act as drones.

The North Indian sitar, the inspiration for this creation, is perhaps the most well-known Indian instrument. The instrument neck in this project is fashioned from cardboard tubing cut lengthwise and mounted to a box with some reinforcement. Here, the movable frets, a feature of the sitar, are nails mounted with rubber bands. Study the photographs for details.

Left *Head of instrument*
Right *Neck/sound box reinforcement*

Double-Tube Lute

Materials

2 cardboard cylinders for sound box body
flat cardboard for soundboard and back
wood stick for neck
small piece of wood (or dowel) for bridge
screw eyes for tuners
strings
nails for hitch pins and optional movable
     frets
larger diameter nail or standard wood nut

Procedure

1 Cut two 4 in segments of 10 in diameter cardboard tubing (see photograph for the interlocking configuration). Mark all areas to be removed for the interlock. Using saw and utility knife, carefully cut until tubes fit snugly together.

2 Find 38 in long wood for the neck. Mark and cut slots into the tube assemblage to receive the neck, as shown.

Another clever way of using cardboard tubes is to interlock two segments together resulting in a more hourglass guitar-like shape. Two tubes of different diameters can be used for more variety of proportion but same diameter tubes are used in this project.

3 Using the tube construction as a pattern, cut out two pieces of sturdy cardboard for the soundboard and back of instrument.

4 Glue neck in place. Glue top and back in place.

5 Attach screw eyes to peg head end. Fix hitch pins or screw eyes to tail end of neck. Screw eyes on both ends allow a greater range of tuning.

6 Optional movable frets using nails and rubber bands require a little effort but upgrade the instrument and make it easier to play once everything is adjusted. Using frets requires a nut which should be

Preparing sound box tubing

Making connecting slots

String length between nut and bridge — 26¼ in. Measure from the nut.

1½ in
2¹³⁄₁₆ in
4⅛ in
5⅜ in
6½ in
7⅝ in
8¹¹⁄₁₆ in
9⅝ in
10½ in
10⁷⁄₁₆ in
12¼ in

Fret placement will approximate this configuration.

Left *Double-tube lute*   Right *East Indian tube-neck lute (p 17)*

slightly higher than the frets. The nut may be either a larger diameter nail than those used for the frets or a standard wood nut with shallow grooves for seating the strings.

7 Based on a string length between nut and bridge of 26¼ in, frets are positioned at distances from the nut, as shown, for a chromatic scale.

8 Apply strings (nylon or metal) and select a small piece of wood or dowel for a bridge.

9 Bring strings up to the desired pitch level. Intervals of unison, octaves, fifths, and fourths are always appropriate. Using different gauges of string will increase the instrument range. The bridge should be high enough so you can play up and down the scale without the strings bumping into frets farther up the fretboard.

This example of lute is made with tubes of different diameters.

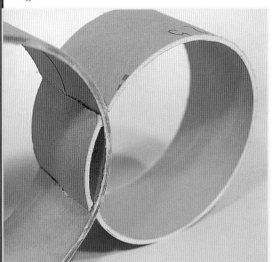

Interlocking tubes   Right *Fitting neck to sound box*

Zithers

Zithers feature a sound box with strings that reach from end to end (or side to side), have no protruding neck, and often, as is the case with psalteries, have no fretboard at all. The size and shape of the box, or its style, determine the number and configuration of strings. Because zithers usually have more strings than guitars, various gauges or thicknesses of string may be necessary—thicker strings for low pitches, thin strings for high pitches.

Shoe Box Zither

The shoe box rubber band harp is a classic homemade instrument. This project is a slightly upgraded design with simple tuners and nylon strings instead of rubber band strings. Box reinforcement is necessary to accommodate the string tension.

Materials

shoe box for sound box body
wood pieces for box reinforcement
nails for hitch pins
screw eyes for tuners
nylon string
dowel bridges

Procedure

1 Cut and glue pieces around interior of box, as shown opposite. The pieces on the ends should be thick enough to receive the hitch pins and tuners.

2 Cut sound hole into top if you wish. Glue top of box to bottom.

3 Cut two lengths of doweling, sand flat on one side, and glue to the top, as shown. Angling one bridge will enhance tuning so that shorter strings will tune higher more easily.

4 Hammer small nails about ¾ in apart along one end and the same with screw eye tuners at the other end, as shown. Use nylon fishing line beginning with the lowest pitches and work your way across making appropriate adjustments as necessary. You may find it expedient to use more than one gauge of string. Strings will generally sound better tuned on the tight side.

Using two hands makes melodies and harmonies easier to play.

Appalachian Zither

This project is based on a simplified Appalachian dulcimer design and will result in an easy-to-play, nice sounding instrument. The diatonic (white key) scale, as shown, makes finding familiar melodies easy.

Materials

proportionally-sized elongated box for sound box body
stick for neck
staple gun and staples for frets
dowels for nut and bridge
music wire
screw eyes for tuners
nails for hitch pins

Procedure

1   Select or modify a box to accommodate the fretboard stick. The one shown is 29½ in long. Sand stick flat and smooth.

2   Mark points for nut, bridge, and frets using fret numbers and the fret distances from nut based on a string length of 27 in between nut and bridge, as shown.

3   Once the nut and bridge are glued into place, the frets may be stapled into the fretboard one by one. Only the melody string is fretted. The other string(s) are drones and do not require frets. Each fret should stand up from the surface of the wood ¹⁄₁₆ in.

4   Attach screw eyes and hitch pin nails to opposite ends of the fretboard.

5   Attach strings. Use lightweight metal strings (gauges .010 to .012).

6   Glue fretboard to box using wood glue or hot glue.

7   Tune strings to the interval of a fifth for standard dulcimer major scale tuning. (Note begins on third fret.) Consult a beginner dulcimer book for tuning options.

8   From the nut, strings should pass close to first frets and increase slightly in trajectory to the bridge. Make height adjustments in the nut, frets, and bridge to set string action and achieve optimum playability.

Top *Staple frets*
Bottom *Screw eye tuners and nut*

Fret placement will approximate this configuration.

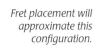

String length between nut and bridge – 27 in. Measure from the nut.
2¾ in
5⅜ in
6⅝ in
8⅞ in
10⅞ in
11¹³⁄₁₆ in
13⅜ in
14⅞ in
16³⁄₁₆ in
16⅞ in
17⅞ in
18⅞ in
19½ in
20⅛ in
20⅞ in
21½ in
21⅞ in

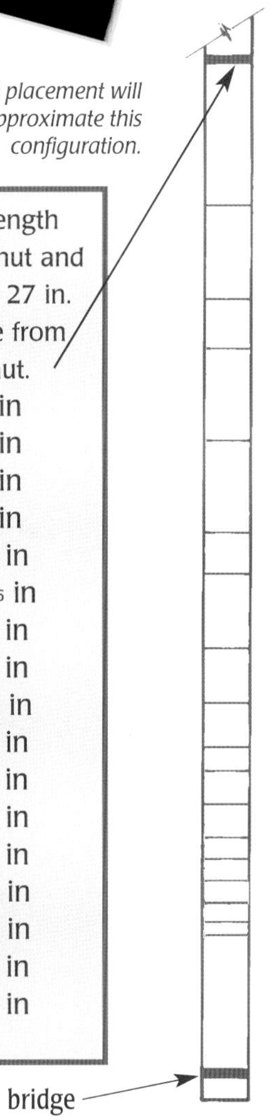

bridge

Asian Zither

This zither idea is prevalent throughout eastern Asia and is loosely based on Japanese koto and Chinese zheng designs which feature an elongated sound box, multiple strings stretching the full length, and movable bridges for tuning. This arrangement allows for pushing the string on the left side of the bridges, as shown, for a special sliding effect. The instrument is characteristically tuned to the five-note, pentatonic scale, somewhat equivalent to the black keys on the piano.

Materials

long box for sound box body
wood for end blocks
bridge material (wood or cardboard tubing)
screw eyes for tuners
nylon string
nails for hitch pins

Procedure

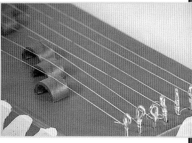

1 Select a sturdy long and shallow box.
2 Measure, cut, and glue wood end blocks in place inside each end of the box to receive tuners and hitch pins. If many strings are planned, use a wood center brace glued between the end blocks on inside of box to keep the box from collapsing as strings are tensioned.
3 Secure box with chosen adhesive so that it is stable and tight.
4 On one end, measure and attach screw eyes spaced 1 in apart so heads do not bump into each other as they are turned.
5 Nail hitch pins on end opposite the screw eyes.
6 Cut a series of center bridges from wood (p 65) or saw small diameter tubing in half, as shown. Bridges should be 1 in to 1½ in tall.
7 Tie nylon strings between hitch pins and tuners. Tighten so that when the bridges are inserted under the strings, the string tension will hold them in place. Bridges remain movable and are never glued to the box.
8 Kotos are usually tuned to a five-note, pentatonic scale by tuning strings to the scale degrees 1−2−3−5−6−8−etc. or to the five black keys on the piano. The relationship between string tension and bridge placement determines various tuning possibilities.

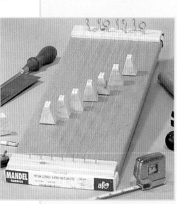

Try using a fabric bolt center for a sound box. Add wood strips at each end, bridges and strings, and play away.

African Tube Zither

This unusual zither is inspired by a Madagascar instrument called the vahila. It is used in various important ceremonies of the Malagasy people.

Materials
cardboard tubes for body and bridges
screw eyes for tuners
nylon strings

Procedure
1 Cut 2½ ft of 3-in-diameter, thick-walled cardboard tubing (carpet tubes or sturdy mailing tubes).
2 For substantial tube material, screw the screw eye tuners directly into it. Otherwise, glue wood end blocks into the ends of the tube to secure tuners.
3 Decide on an appropriate number of strings and their configuration (strings can entirely or partially surround the tube).
4 Insert screw eyes on opposing ends, as shown, and begin securing strings between screw eye pairs. Consider decorating the tube before stringing.
5 Movable bridges are cut from small diameter cardboard tubing and short nails are secured to each bridge by rubber bands (as shown below) to provide a more positive point of contact and reinforcement.
6 Space bridges in a spiral configuration around the tube creating short to long string lengths. Because bridges are movable for finding suitable pitches, all the strings should tighten to about the same degree.
7 Cradle the instrument in both hands, as shown below, prop the instrument in a comfortable position against your body or on your lap, and pluck strings with your fingers.

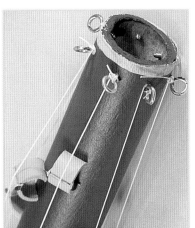

Experiment with bridge placements. Use small nails and rubber bands to reinforce the cardboard tube bridges.

Correct playing position

23

East Indian Zither

The classical veena of India produces some of the most interesting sounding music in the world. As with the Indian sitar, it is still revered and played today. This project is a highly simplified version of the instrument.

Materials

cardboard tube for neck
small cylindrical cardboard containers for resonators
wood for end blocks
nuts and bolts
screw eyes for tuners
metal strings
nails for frets
rubber bands

Procedure

1 Cut a 24 in length of 3-in-diameter tube lengthwise, as shown below, with a sharp hand saw or band saw. This is the neck.

2 Cut and glue wood end blocks onto the ends of the tube, as shown.

3 Find two containers and place them several inches from each end of the tube. Drill holes in tube and container lids and secure together with small nuts and bolts, as shown. Big washers on the nut/bolt connection will help to stabilize the overall assemblage. Fit cans to lids.

4 Use 3½ in nails held on with rubber bands for the movable frets. Use slightly larger nails for the nut and bridge. Optionally, the height of the bridge can be made adjustable by using small screw eyes, as shown.

5 Attach screw eye tuners to each end block (for a greater range of tuning).

6 Use lightweight metal guitar strings (two thin diameter strings .010 in and one thicker gauge .020 in wound). Tie strings to their respective tuners and tension until the sound becomes resonant. Use an interval of a fifth between the thick string and two thinner unison strings.

7 Any number of tunings are possible, especially since the frets themselves are movable. Move the frets until a recognizable scale is achieved.

8 Lay the instrument across your lap or shoulder, as shown, and pluck with fingertips or pick. A characteristic sliding or bending effect can be produced by holding a string down and pushing it across the fret, thus raising the pitch in the process.

Below left End block and fret
Right Attaching container to neck
Bottom Tuners and "adjustable" bridge

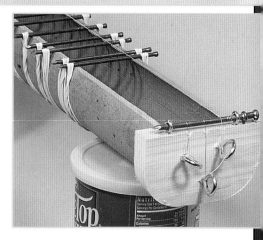

Harps

Harps are plucked stringed instruments with strings that run obliquely to the sound box. Most all world cultures possess some kind of harp. Angle and arch (also called bow) harps are typical in African and some Asian countries while triangular frame harp construction is more common in Europe.

Angle Harp

Harps made in the form of an angle between the sound box and string bearing component were probably precursors to the more familiar triangular form we see today.

Materials
cardboard box for sound box body
2 sticks of wood for frame
bolts and nuts
nylon strings
screw eyes or other tuning mechanisms

Procedure

1 Select a sturdy box. Measure and cut the box so that a 1½ in x ¾ in wood stick (called a string rib) passes through the box, as shown. Stick should protrude about 2 in on either end. Cut a hole into the back of the box for access to the inside for stringing or repair.

2 Attach the other stick (neck) of wood to form an elbow, as shown. Screw or bolt sticks together. Glue will help stabilize this important junction.

3 Put stick assemblage and box together and project the path of the strings between them. This construction does not allow for too many strings as excessive tension may cause damage to the instrument. Strings should be about ¾ in apart, as shown.

4 Drill holes through both the box and inside string rib stick for each string. After double checking string trajectories and spacings, place screw eye tuners along the neck. Attach strings from the inside of the box using a knot to secure this end. Pass other end of string through string rib and the face of the box and tie to its respective tuner. Slowly bring up tension of strings.

5 Tune to basic do-re-mi major scale.

6 Hold, as shown above , to play.

Connecting neck and string rib

Drilling string holes

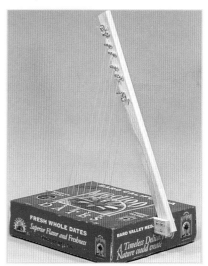

Irish Harp

The Irish harp (also called Celtic harp and clarsach) features a triangular framework attached to a sound box. The Celtic harp has become a symbol of Irish culture.

Materials

cardboard box for sound box body
3 sticks of wood for frame
thin flat piece of wood for string rib support
bolts, nuts and washers
nylon strings
screw eyes or other tuning mechanisms

Procedure

1 Use a slightly elongated box. Cut one to size, if necessary.

2 Glue a string rib support, as shown below, to the face of the sound box to anchor and stabilize the wood frame which will eventually be glued to the box.

3 This project is similar to the angle harp except that three pieces of wood are used (string rib, neck, and pillar) to form a closed triangle making the structure stronger to withstand more string tension. The framework is then glued to the outside of the box rather than going through the box. Lay out wood to approximate the configuration shown in the photographs. For proper string alignment, add a wood shim at the juncture between the neck and pillar, as shown on p 27.

4 Bolt and glue framework together.

5 Determine the number and trajectory of strings from the string rib to the tuners along the neck. Strings should be about ½ to ¾ in apart. Drill holes through the side of the string rib for anchoring strings.

6 Now glue the string rib component of the assembled framework securely to the foundational wood strip which

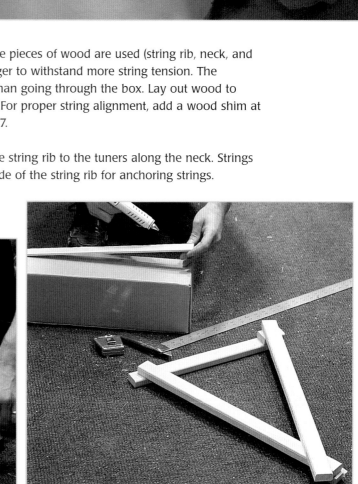

Preparing harp sound box and frame

Gluing rib support to sound box and frame configuration

was previously glued onto the sound box, as shown below.

7 Attach screw eye tuners.

8 Since this instrument uses more than four or five strings, different gauges of string may be necessary for a good sounding scale. Thicker, longer strings are used in the low or bass end and thinner, shorter strings for high-sounding pitches.

9 Harps are usually tuned to a standard do-re-mi major scale. It usually takes several tuning sessions before the strings settle in and hold their pitches.

Triangular wood framework is glued and bolted for strength.

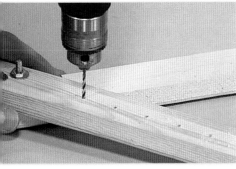

Drilling holes through side of string rib for attaching strings

Above *Shim added for better string alignment*

Left *Framework glued to sound box*

African Harp

The kora was used in African cultures to pass down traditions and mores through song and playing. The design of two parallel string sets allows interesting melodic and rhythmic techniques.

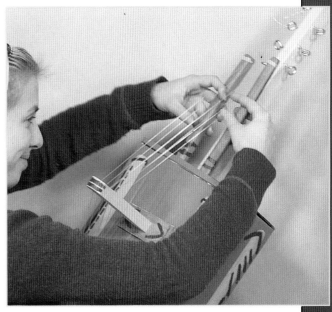

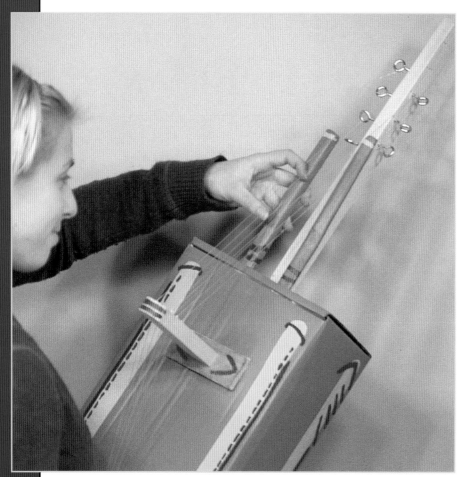

Materials

sturdy, medium-size box for sound box body
2 dowels or pieces of broom stick for handles
long flat stick for neck
wood pieces for bridge and bridge platform
screw eyes for tuners
nylon string

Procedure

1 The placement of the neck (¾ in x 1½ in x 32 in) and the two ¾-in dowel handles on either side of the neck should be marked onto the box. The dowels should be long enough to go completely through the box and protrude an additional 7 or 8 in and close enough to the neck so the strings are within easy reach of the index finger and thumb, as shown on p 29.

2 Cut holes in box and insert the three wood components. The neck should lie back an additional 1½ in from the plane of the soundboard for good string alignment and accessibility for fingers.

3 Attach a number of good size screw eyes on either side of the neck about 1½ in apart. Stagger the tuners, as shown. The position of the first tuner is located 8 in from the sound box so its string will not bump into the box on the way to the bridge.

4 Make the vertical bridge from a 6 in scrap of ¾ in x 1½ in wood. Saw grooves or shallow notches along the edges of the bridge beginning 3 in from the surface of the soundboard. Space additional notches ½ in apart. Using a long ruler, check the path of the strings as they pass through the bridge notches and onto the tuners, making sure they are free from obstruction.

5 Strings tie off at the tail piece end of the

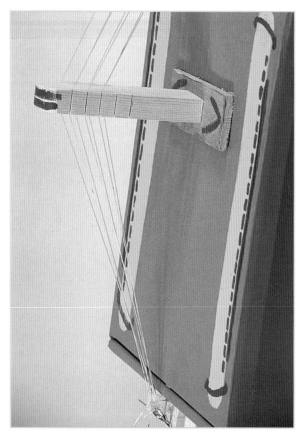

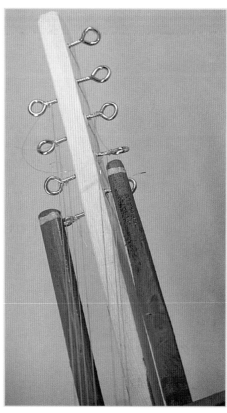

instrument. They should be well-anchored since this number of strings can exert a great deal of pulling power.

6 Since the top soundboard portion of the box is vulnerable to the down-bearing pressure of the bridge, a thin foundation platform for the bridge can be positioned and glued to the box to help protect the box and distribute the vibrations.

7 Attach nylon strings from tailpiece, through their respective bridge notches, and onto their respective screw eyes where they are secured for tuning. Depending on number of strings, three or four gauges of string may be necessary to create a smooth sounding scale. Make adjustments as necessary.

8 Tune strings on opposing sides of the neck to the same pitch. This arrangement facilitates interesting rhythmic possibilities between the hands.

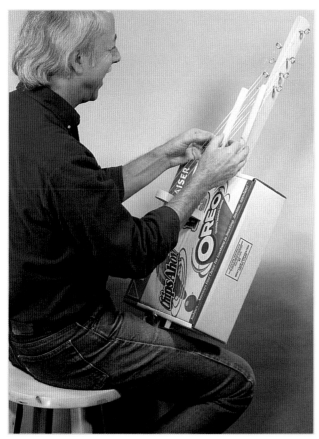

Strings should be accessible to the thumbs and first fingers for easy playing.

Lyres

Two different arrangements of this ancient instrument are shown here, one made from a pizza box, the other from a produce box. Both use the same characteristic framework configuration.

Top *Produce box used for sound box body*
Bottom *A pizza box sound box body*

Materials

cardboard box for sound box body
wood sticks for string-bearing framework
wood screws
nylon string
screw eyes or other tuning mechanisms
pieces of wood for bridge

Procedure

1 Use a medium-size box for the lyre body and decide how you would like to configure the wood to the box (see photograph for different styles).

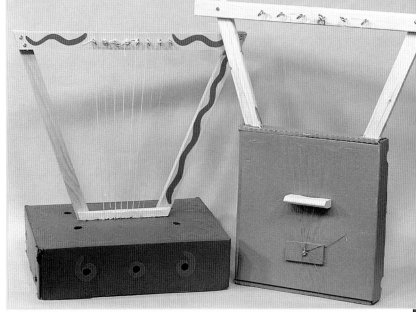

2 The string-bearing framework requires four different lengths of wood fastened together to form the characteristic lyre shape. Cut sticks to size to suit the box.

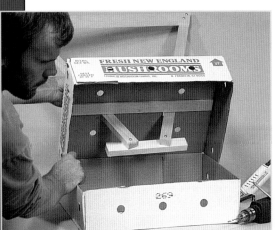

3 Attach framework to the box. The free-standing design requires a supporting brace glued to the inside of the box which is accessed by cutting a hole in the back of the box or using box lid, as shown at left. The flat pizza-style box also needs a reinforcing block of wood, as seen on the lower right, for anchoring the strings. Mark and cut the box to receive the framework. Make adjustments as necessary.

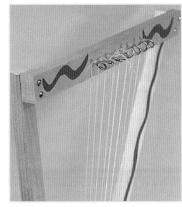

4 Screw framework together. Some pieces may need to be inserted into the interior of the box before screwing the entire frame together.

5 The free-standing design requires additional bracing on top surface of box, as shown on right, for extra stability. Now drill string holes ½ in apart into the top, as shown. The other model needs only an extra screw to act as a hitch pin for string anchorage, as well as a separate bridge, see bottom right.

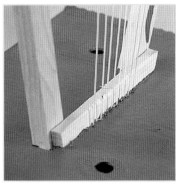

6 Attach screw eyes and strings. The pizza box lyre requires a bridge between strings and sound box. Bring strings up to pitch. Lyres are usually tuned to a standard scale.

Top left Interior brace of freestanding lyre

Middle right Extra brace on freestanding lyre
Bottom right Bridge and hitch pin arrangement on flat lyre

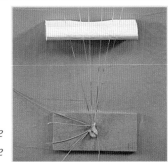

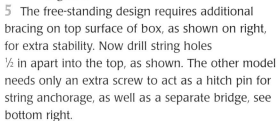

String Basses

Bass instruments with long, large-diameter strings are specifically designed for producing low pitches. Strings coupled with a big box increase the resonance to an impressive degree. These designs have amazingly good sound.

Materials

cardboard box for sound
     box body
2x4 lumber for neck
weed trimmer string
screw eyes or other tuning mechanisms
nails for hitch pins
piece of wood for bridge

Procedure

1 Cut 5 ft of 2x4.

2 Decide where the 2x4 will spike through the box. Keep the 2x4 up close to the face or soundboard of the instrument to help set the action, keeping the strings close enough to the playing face for easy fingering, as shown. A slightly more complex design option modifies the box, as shown in the diagram, and sets the neck at an angle making the strings less likely to bump into the box.

3 Carefully cut holes through the box and insert 2x4. Decide where to position the box along the neck length and use duct tape to secure it.

4 Decide how many strings to mount (two or three) and hammer nails in the tail end of the instrument. Attach tuners on the other end.

5 Select a couple of gauges of weed trimmer line, tie one end securely to the nail and attach other end to tuner. Take up the slack.

6 Make a bridge approximately 2 in high and notch it to help seat the strings and keep them from slipping around when you play. Place bridge between strings and sound box.

7 Tension strings to desired pitches. Find the lowest pitch where the lowest sounding string begins to resonate. Use this as a reference to tune the next string to a unison pitch or a fourth or fifth higher. Adjust everything higher or lower, as necessary.

8 Experiment with bridge placement for the best sound.

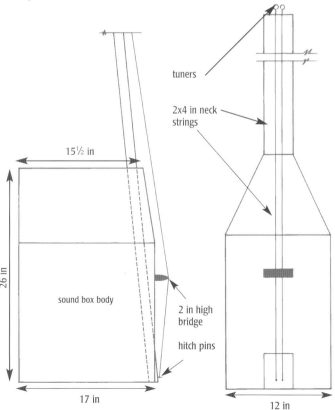

tuners

2x4 in neck
strings

15½ in

26 in

sound box body

2 in high
bridge

hitch pins

17 in

12 in

Wind Instruments (Aerophones)

Wind instruments (aerophones) can be made from various types of smaller-diameter cardboard tubes, providing they are protected from moisture. Paper roll tubes, mailing tubes, carpet tubes, tubing used in the construction industry, and tubing available through hobby stores and craft outlets all have potential for instrument projects. Other high-tech kinds of tubing made of highly compressed layers of cardboard do not require moisture protection. The basic acoustic principle with all wind instruments is that longer tubes produce lower pitches, shorter ones make higher sounds.

Digeridoo

This fascinating Australian aboriginal instrument has become a cultural symbol for its originators and popular in some kinds of contemporary world music. Its low resonant drone, produced by loosely buzzing the lips into the tube, is enhanced through more advanced techniques such as circular breathing and the practice of superimposing various vocalized inflections on the fundamental drone pitch.

Procedure

1 Cut 4 to 5 ft of ½- to 1-in-diameter cardboard tubing.
2 Decorate with various designs and colors.
3 Finish with a nontoxic, moisture-resistant product (use a swab for inside) to protect the cardboard from absorbing too much moisture as it is played.
4 Find someone to demonstrate digeridoo playing technique. Basically, puff out your cheeks and flubber your lips into the tube. Try to find the lowest, most resonant note possible. While buzzing your lips, make vocal sounds for unusual textures. Ultimately, learn to circular breath (taking a snatch of breath while blowing at the same time) to produce a continuous, unbroken drone.

Trumpets

Different lengths of tubing will produce different pitches. With longer tubes of relatively small diameter, by tightening and loosening your lips as you buzz them, you may be able to make several different pitches. Bugles and other keyless trumpets work on this principle.

Procedure

1 Cut desired length of small diameter tube. Try playing like a trumpet by tightly buzzing or vibrating your lips into one end of the tube while blowing with strong lung pressure. Experiment with different lengths. You may be able to get more than one note by tightening or loosening your lips. It is easier to elicit this spectrum of notes called the "overtone series" from a longer section of tubing. Add a bell shape onto the tube for better look and sound enhancement.
2 Optionally, make a simple trombone from long tubes of slightly different diameters so that they fit snugly one into the other. By telescoping the tubes short to long, different notes can be achieved.

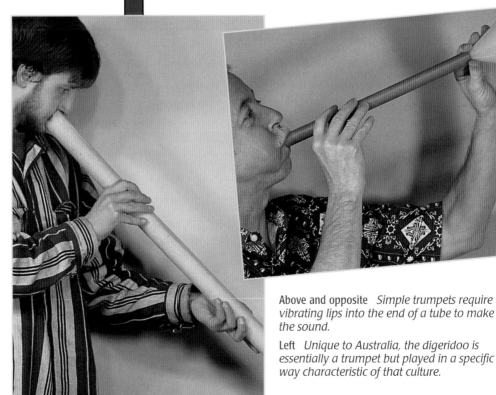

Above and opposite *Simple trumpets require vibrating lips into the end of a tube to make the sound.*

Left *Unique to Australia, the digeridoo is essentially a trumpet but played in a specific way characteristic of that culture.*

Flutes

Flutes are among the most universal of instruments and were traditionally made from bamboo and reeds. Cardboard tubes with small diameters can be used to make different types of flutes.

Procedure

1 Make a transverse flute (below) from 12 in of compressed ½- to ¾-in-diameter tubing. Tightly plug one end with a cork. Drill a ⅜ in hole 1 in from that end for the blowing hole. This hole must be neat for easy tone production.

2 After making a sound, begin drilling ¼ in fingerholes starting about 2 in from the end opposite the blowing hole. Each successive fingerhole should be about 1 in distance from the previous one. Fingerholes should not be drilled too close to the blowing hole as this will undermine the flute's playability.

3 If you find it difficult to produce a sound, ask a flute player to help you get started.

4 Pan flutes (or panpipes) are a series of small diameter tubes of different lengths, tightly stopped or plugged on one end, and bundled together for easy handling.

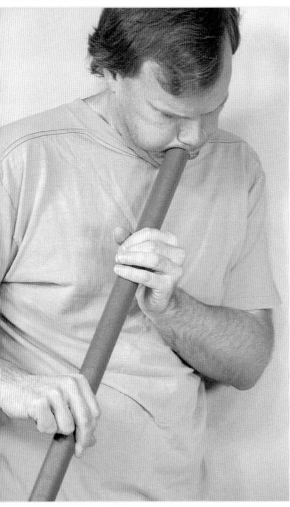

Top *Proper playing position for transverse flute*

Bottom *Panpipes*

Simple Box Drum Set

Arrange and stack a selection of different-size boxes around a chair for an instant drum set. Generous application of duct tape or other adhesive will help hold it all together while you beat out rhythms with drumsticks. Needless to say, most boxes will take only so much punishment before falling apart. Perhaps that is part of the fun.

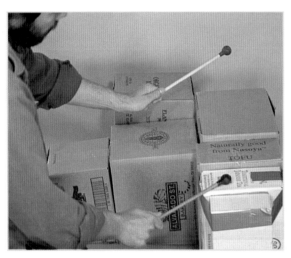

Twirling Drums

Glue two heavy-duty paper picnic plates together for the body, or use a segment of cardboard tubing with a cardboard front and back. For a handle, add a stick or piece of dowel and attach two beads on strings at the sides, as shown. Note   Stick and beads should be securely attached to body so they will not come apart in the playing. Rotate apparatus so beads flip-flop against drum heads to make the sound.

Heavy-duty picnic plates glued together or pieces of cardboard glued to a segment of cardboard tubing make instant twirling drums when a handle and beads on a string are attached.

Boom Tubes/Percussion Tubes

Boom tubes, shown at right, are open-ended, thin-walled cardboard tubes (gift wrapping or paper towel cores) which when struck against most any object emit a resonant pitch depending on their relative lengths.

Percussion tubes are made by tightly closing one end of a long tube and either clapping your hands close to the open end or striking the open end with a flat object such as a flip flop sandal. A surprisingly resonant sound results. Different lengths of tube produce different specific pitches.

BooBams

BooBams are fashioned from medium to large diameter tubing cut to different lengths with one end covered with thin resilient material. Glue thin plywood or attach heavy balloon rubber or innertube tire onto one end of a tube, then strike it with sticks or hands or various types of mallets to create a great resonant sound. Clustering tubes of different lengths together increases the rhythmic and melodic possibilities.

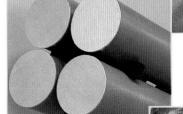

Saw large diameter cardbord tubes to various lengths to produce different resonances.

Stamping Tubes

Stamping tubes are fashioned from 4 to 5 ft of medium diameter tubing with substantial wall thickness. The tubes are tightly capped and secured with some very resilient material on one end. This end is stamped vertically against the floor. The other end is left open. Dropping the closed end of the tube on the earth or slightly cushioned floor causes an interesting resonant sound. Different lengths of tubing produce different pitches.

Drums

Cardboard tubes of various diameters lend themselves readily to making drums. All that needs to be added is the drum head.

Procedure

1 The easiest construction is to glue a thin piece of ⅛ in plywood securely over a length of tubing.

2 Another simple solution is to pull heavy-duty packing tape tightly across one end of tubing to completely cover the opening. Pencil-like drumsticks elicit the best sound.

3 Innertube rubber or other stretchy material strong enough to be laced also works well. Before mounting the heads you can wrap the cardboard tube in decorative paper (cloth works too) for a different look.

4 Make bongo drums by fastening short tubes of contrasting lengths together.

5 Drums using animal skin or rawhide require a more complicated procedure that is beyond the scope of this book.

Rattles and Rainsticks

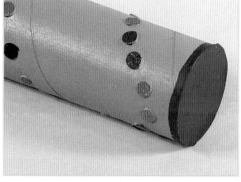

Rattles are used universally, often in ceremonial or ritual contexts. Rainsticks are used for rain magic. Rattles and rainsticks were traditionally made from bamboo, gourds, cactus branches, and other natural materials. The projects here are made from mailing tubes and paper roll tubes.

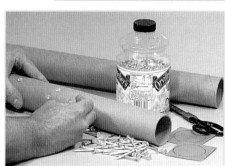

Procedure

1 To make a simple tube rattle place a quantity of different rattling materials inside the tube and secure the ends.

2 To make a rainstick, perforate a 2 to 4 ft length of tubing with an array of nails (aluminum roofing nails with large heads and slightly shorter than the tube diameter are best). Create the "rain" effect, by filling one quarter of the length of the tube with beans, peas, corn, pebbles, or seeds. Slowly flip the tube end to end and inside materials will gently clatter through nails.

3 Once you're satisfied with the sound, close the ends securely with the caps provided by the manufacturer, or glue thin plywood on each end, or seal with packing tape.

Xylophones

Almost all cultures have some form of xylophone, called marimba in Latin America. The instruments in this book feature keys made from wood or metal, and a stand fashioned from cardboard.

Procedure for three possibilities

1 Lay scraps of wood of any type across a couple of cardboard boxes. Strike with various sticks, unpadded and padded, and note the keys that make the most attractive sounds. Generally, thinner pieces of wood give a lower sound.

2 Another very simple staircase xylophone frame may be cut from flat cardboard, as shown. Use copper tubing for keys. Each key should be slightly padded where it touches the frame for the best results.

3 For a more sophisticated xylophone, find a stick of wood with no splits or knots or a length of ¾ in copper or aluminum tubing. Cut different lengths to get some sense of the relationship between length and pitch. To elicit the clearest pitch, arrange keys on some soft or spongy material that touches only at each key's nodes. To find the node points (points of no vibration) on each key, measure approximately one quarter of the overall length (22½ percent to be more exact) from each end. As the keys are lined up, the nodes will ultimately determine the shape of the supporting framework. Experiment with ways to modify a box to accommodate the node arrangement and keep each key in place.

Try different mallets.

22½ %   loop   22½ %

node   node

22½ %
in from
total length   xylophone stand   22½ %
in from
total length

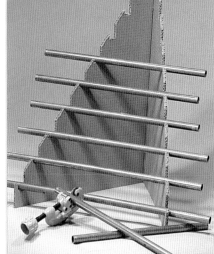

Above *Wood scraps across cardboard boxes*

Left *Copper tubing across cardboard staircase configuration*

37

Example of modified box to accommodate wood keys

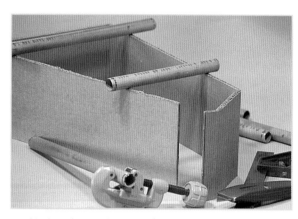

Node points on lengths of metal tubing determine configuration of the stand.

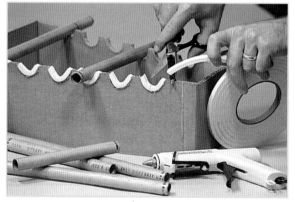

Padding under each key makes them sound better.

Tuning—arranging keys from long to short—low to high

Try different mallets for a variety of sounds.

African Thumb Piano

This unique instrument is modeled after the African mbira (also called sanza, likembe, and kalimba). It is played for ceremonial purposes as well as for fun. It's said that the mbira was used for relaying messages during slave times. Thumb pianos come in all shapes and sizes with any number of keys. Some varieties are held inside a large gourd or other container for added resonance.

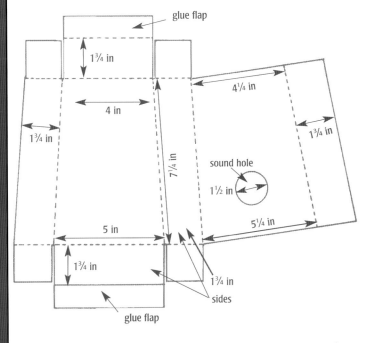

glue flap

1¾ in

4 in

4¼ in

1¾ in

1¾ in

7¼ in

sound hole

1½ in

5¼ in

5 in

1¾ in

1¾ in

sides

glue flap

Materials

flat cardboard for sound box body
doweling for bridge assembly
thin plywood for bridge foundation plate
2 screws and matching T-nuts
some "springy" tongues of metal or wood (leaf rake tines
    or most any kind of flattened steel or spring steel)

Procedure

1 Plot pattern on flat cardboard and cut out. Incise, crimp, and fold (p 41) into shape.
2 Cut a piece of thin plywood to act as the platform for the bridge and key assemblage. A slightly larger platform of hardwood will provide more resonance.
3 Cut a portion of the dowel in half lengthwise and glue pieces to platform. Study diagram and photos on p 40.
4 Place down-bearing dowel component in place and drill holes through it and the platform.
5 Glue the top assemblage to the sound box.
6 Push screws through down-bearing dowel and

Side view of paper plate mbira

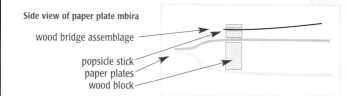

wood bridge assemblage
popsicle stick
paper plates
wood block

Paper Plate Thumb Piano

1 Glue wood block between two plates to help stabilize key assemblage. Glue plates together.

2 Popsicle sticks are sandwiched between two wood strips which act as a bridge. Cut sticks to different lengths.

3 The bridge/key assembly is then glued to the plate assembly directly on top of the interior wood block.

cardboard. Attach T-nuts onto screws and seat them securely into place.

7 Glue box together.

8 Cut tongues to length (approx. 3 to 4 in for metal). Sand off all sharp edges and corners and place tongues at even intervals across box.

9 Carefully screw the down-bearing strip on top of the tongues until they begin to produce a clear pitch.

10 Before screws are tightened snug, adjust the tongues to match a scale by varying the length of the vibrating portion.

11 Hold the thumb piano in both hands, as shown below, with thumbs plucking the tongues singly or in combinations to make melodies.

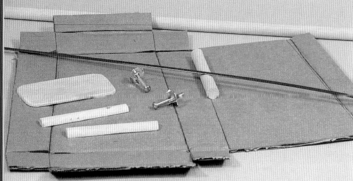

side view

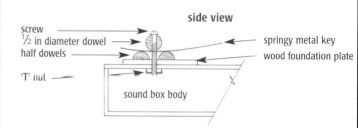

screw
½ in diameter dowel
half dowels
'T' nut
sound box body
springy metal key
wood foundation plate

Detail photographs showing bridge assembly

Below *Holding position of mbira*

40

Part 2 Designing and Building More Complex Instruments

Stringed Instruments (Chordophones)

Sound Box Design

Building boxes of various shapes from scratch poses a fun challenge. In some cases it is easiest to cut separate parts and then glue (or tape) them together as one would do with woodworking. But you become a box-master when you can cut an entire sound box in one piece and fold it into shape. Several examples of this approach are demonstrated in this section of the book. Simply transfer the pattern measurements to a section of cardboard and cut out. Stiffer grades of cardboard will usually require crimping (a light incision along the dotted line of the fold on the inside with a knife), before it will fold neatly. Be careful not to cut through to the outside. Drag a dull, rounded object along the line to crush the cardboard so that when folded, it forms a neat crease on the outside.

Use a basic square or rectangular box shape or a trapezoid. This requires careful measuring, cutting, and folding, but makes a more attractive instrument and is worth the extra effort. Use the diagram for the basic design and measurements. The measurements can be adjusted to accommodate whatever size and proportion you require.

A viable alternative for easy sound box construction is to use large diameter cardboard construction tubing. Consult local home center or hardware stores for suggested access to this resource. Thick walled tubing is best but it may be slightly harder to work with. A small saw and sharp utility knife are the necessary tools.

The primary construction principle for the instruments in this section is that necks and framework, not the cardboard sound box, bear the tension caused by tightened strings. Necks and framework should attach passively to the cardboard elements putting as little stress as possible on the cardboard itself.

Many of the following projects, although still made primarily of cardboard, utilize more wood construction than projects in Part 1 of this book. Inexpensive softwoods, hardwoods, and plywoods work well. The projects can be constructed with basic carpenter tools. The use of some specialty and power tools can also be helpful (p 6).

Measuring and cutting cardboard

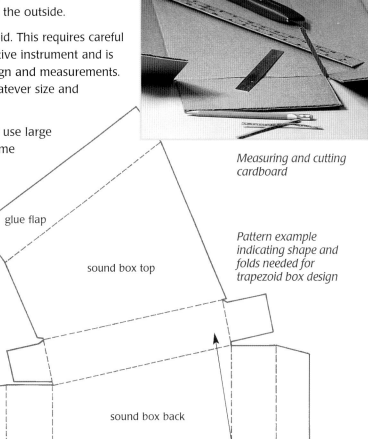

Pattern example indicating shape and folds needed for trapezoid box design

glue flap

sound box top

sound box back

sides

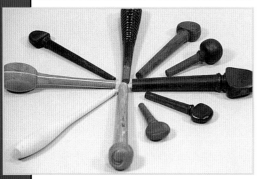

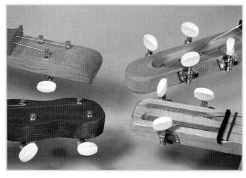

Tuners and Peg Head Design

As the projects gradually increase in complexity, a defined string length, better tuning mechanisms, and fret placement become more important. The string length is determined by the distance between the inside of the nut (the defining element at the peg head of the instrument) and the inside of the bridge (the defining element at the soundboard). For more complex instruments, machine tuners and zither pins are used for precision tuning. Inexpensive machine tuners can be found or ordered through any music instrument store. Zither pins are a type of finely threaded tuner commonly found on autoharps, hammered dulcimers, and small folk

Styles of tuning mechanisms and peg head designs
Top left *machine tuners*
Top right *zither pins*
Bottom left *friction pegs*
Bottom right *peg head designs*

harps. These require some precision drilling and a matching tuning wrench to make them work. Friction pegs (found on violins) are also viable but require careful fitting.

Good peg head design is crucial to insure that the instrument tunes and plays properly. The type of tuners used should match the instrument's design, especially the peg head. Purchase tuners early in the building process and fashion the peg head to suit the tuner. Several ideas for peg head design are offered in this section. The following basic design is easy to make and should accommodate any guitar-style instrument.

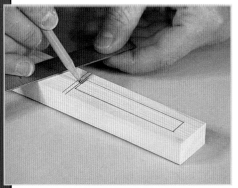

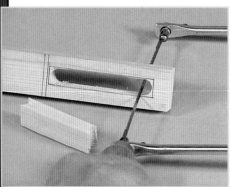

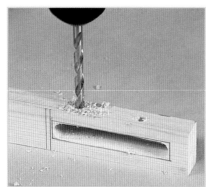

Procedure

1 Choose an appropriate-size piece of wood for the neck/peg head and mark major points of reference based on string length including nut and bridge placement, hitch pin arrangement, and peg head preparation.

2 Draw the peg head design, as shown. Adjust design as necessary depending on number of strings, string paths from nut to tuners, tuner requirements, and aesthetic considerations.

3 Drill and cut out peg slot, as shown. File and sand to uniformity.

4 Space actual tuners onto peg head for exact positioning. Remember that there is a difference between machine tuners that mount to the right side and those machined for the left side of the peg head so they will turn the correct way while tuning the strings. Mark any holes for drilling.

Hardwoods usually require pre-drilling small holes for the little screws which hold the tuners to the peg head. Double check all measurements and drill holes, as shown.

5 Cut slot for the nut, as shown.

6 On completion of the instrument, attach tuners, as shown, and string appropriately.

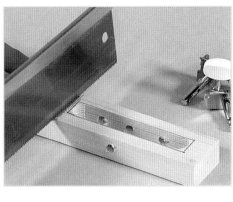

Fretting

Fretting determines the playability of the instrument. Professionals use a wide variety of fret wire based on precision measurements necessary to accommodate the requirements of different instruments. For this project use a standard size guitar or banjo fret wire (it will work on most any instrument). Refer to the photographs for the basic process of installing music fret wire on a fretboard. Note some frets are installed directly into the neck, whereas others are installed into a separate fretboard that is then glued onto the neck for a more finished look.

Procedure

1 Determine the exact string length between nut and bridge. This dictates the placement of frets along the fingerboard. Use an existing instrument as a model or find your own fret placements by using the Rule of Eighteen (or the integer 17.817). Divide the string length by 17.817 to find the distance from the nut to the first fret. The remaining distance divided by 17.817 gives the distance from the first fret to the second fret. And so forth. A calculator helps. This formula will give a chromatic scale (all semitones the same as all the black and white keys on a piano). When the calculations are finished, make a master template for future use. There is also a computer software available for fret placement figuring.

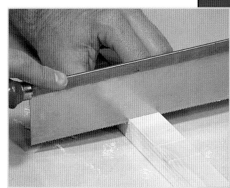

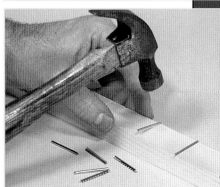

2 After determining exact string length and calculating fret placement along the fretboard, mark these as precisely as possible with a sharp pencil, as shown.

3 Using a speciality saw or one with an appropriate set to the teeth, cut shallow grooves for receiving each fret, as shown. Practice on a scrap piece of wood first.

4 Cut the frets to length and hammer them firmly but carefully into the slots, as shown. If they loosen, use a little epoxy glue to help secure them.

5 Being careful not to loosen the fret too much, file any extra overhang until it is flush with the side of the fretboard. Then carefully round the ends of the frets to eliminate any sharp points or edges, as shown.

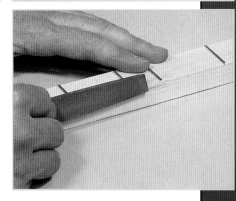

Lutes, Guitars, Banjos

Guitars and other members of the lute branch of the chordophone instrument family in this book all share certain construction principles defined by a neck or fingerboard usually with frets, a body or sound box of various shapes, sizes, and construction materials, purchased tuning mechanisms, and any number of strings, usually from two to six. The basic two-component design of neck and sound box makes this kind of instrument easy to build using cardboard and wood construction.

Russian Lute

The pattern for this instrument is inspired by the balalaika, a popular traditional folk stringed instrument of Russia.

Materials

flat cardboard for sound box body
wood for neck
small wood pieces for nut and bridge
screw eyes and nails for tuners and hitch pins
string

Procedure

1 Plot the trapezoidal pattern measurements on a piece of plain cardboard (double or single ply). Adjust pattern to suit the dimensions of the wood you've chosen for the neck (should be same width as neck wood).

2 Cut, crimp, and fold (p 41) sound box. Begin to modify the sound box as necessary to accommodate the neck.

3 Adding an optional fingerboard to the neck will help smooth out the fingerboard/sound box junction. The addition of a nut also helps define a more specific string length and aids in tuning. The nut may be inserted in a slot on the fingerboard (p 43) or simply glued onto the fingerboard.

4 Glue or tape the box together. Join the neck/fingerboard assemblage to the sound box. Make necessary adjustments for a good fit. Secure with glue or tape.

5 Add screw eyes for tuners, and nails (or more screw eyes) at the other end. Other tuners may be used if you choose.

6 Attach nylon or metal strings. Remember that thicker strings for lower pitches create more tension on the instrument. Experiment with different gauges.

7 Tune strings to desired intervals.

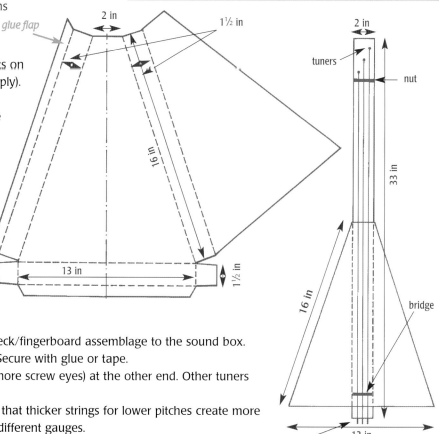

3-String Dulcitar

The dulcitar is a cross between a fretted dulcimer and a guitar. Its do-re-mi scale and familiar holding position make it one of the easiest instruments to play. With only two or three strings, dulcimer-related instruments are usually played with one string acting as a melody string and the others as drones. This instrument project uses the more functional machine tuners and real frets.

Materials

flat cardboard for sound box body
wood for neck
wood pieces for nut and bridge
strings
fret wire
machine tuners
nails for hitch pins

Procedure

1 Plot the trapezoidal pattern measurements of sound box body onto flat cardboard. This design has the advantage of hiding the primary box fold under the neck for a more seamless look.

2 Carefully cut out pattern. Mark, cut, crimp, and fold (p 41) cardboard into box shape. Make any modifications necessary. Do not glue box together until after fretboard is made in case of adjustments. Make nut and bridge.

3 Study the accompanying fretboard design and photographs and transfer all measurements to the wood neck based on a string length (between nut and bridge) of 23½ in. Remember that the following fret pattern is for a standard do-re-mi or diatonic scale, not a chromatic scale as found on guitars.

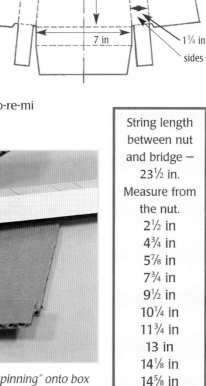

fold in flaps
5 in
10 in
7 in
1¾ in
sides

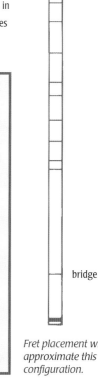

nut

bridge

Fret placement will approximate this configuration.

String length between nut and bridge — 23½ in. Measure from the nut.
2½ in
4¾ in
5⅞ in
7¾ in
9½ in
10¼ in
11¾ in
13 in
14⅛ in
14⅝ in

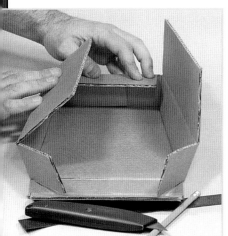

Folding dulcitar box

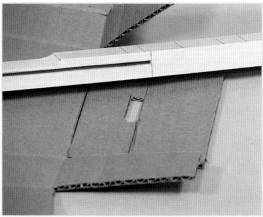

Preparing neck slot for "clothespinning" onto box

4 Using the tuners as a guide, mark the peg head slot. Drill and saw (p 42). File and sand to specification.

5 Cut shallow slots for the nut and bridge. Drill three small holes at the tail end, as shown, for securing strings. Strings with ball ends instead of loop ends work best for this arrangement.

6 Jigsaw or band saw the long slot in neck wood, as shown, which will clothespin onto the sound box. Cut and file a strum hollow into the fretboard. Fit the neck to the sound box making any necessary adjustments. Do not glue yet.

7 Using the measurements given here or the *Rule of Eighteen* (p 43), plot fret placements and carefully install frets into sawed slots (p 43).

8 In stages, glue box and fretboard together placing glue on all points of contact.

9 Attach strings. Use standard guitar strings of the following gauges: middle and melody strings—.010 in; bass string—.020 in wound.

10 The strings at the nut should be slightly higher than the first fret. The bridge should be high enough so you can play up and down the scale without strings hitting any obstruction.

11 Tune to standard dulcimer tunings. For a major scale, try tuning the bass string to a D and the other two higher strings to an A. "Do" begins at the third fret on the melody string. Other great tunings can be found in dulcimer song books.

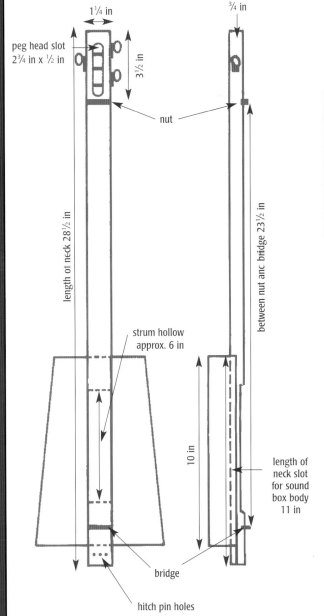

peg head slot
2¾ in x ½ in

1¼ in

¾ in

3½ in

nut

length of neck 28½ in

between nut and bridge 23½ in

strum hollow
approx. 6 in

10 in

length of neck slot for sound box body 11 in

bridge

hitch pin holes

Making peg head

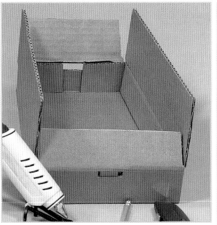

Above *Gluing box with hot glue*
The front flaps do not overlap.
They butt together and are hidden under the neck.

Right *Drilling holes in tailpiece for hitching strings.*

3-String Guitar

When brought to the Americas, the Spanish guitar underwent various modifications and today is found in many variant forms throughout Latin America. The tres (three strings) is found primarily in Cuba, Dominican Republic, and Puerto Rico, although sometimes the number of strings is doubled for a more vibrant sound. For this project use a modified trapezoid box design.

Materials

flat cardboard for sound box body
wood for neck
wood pieces for nut and bridge
music wire for strings
fret wire
machine tuners

Procedure

1 Plot the trapezoidal pattern measurements onto flat cardboard.

2 Carefully cut out design. Mark, cut, crimp, and fold (p 41) cardboard into box shape, as shown. Make any modifications necessary.

3 Study the wood neck design and transfer all dimensions to the neck stock and cut to size. Round back of neck for comfortable playing.

4 Using tuners as a guide, mark the peg head and cut to the suggested configuration (p 42). Drill holes to accommodate the tuners. File and sand to specification.

5 At the opposite end of the neck, jigsaw the long slot which will clothespin onto the sound box, as shown. Fit the neck to the sound box making adjustments as you go.

6 Drill three small holes at the tail end for securing strings. Ball end strings work best.

7 Using the measurements given or the *Rule of Eighteen* (p 43), plot fret placements, saw slots, and carefully

Folding cardboard for sound box

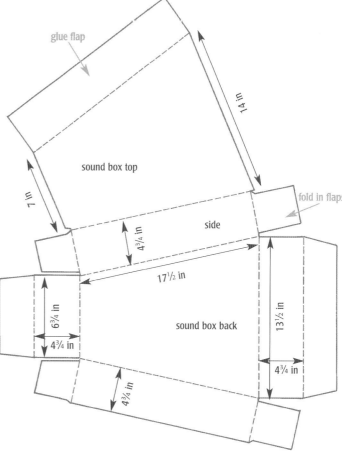

glue flap

14 in

sound box top

7 in

4¾ in

side

fold in flaps

17½ in

13½ in

sound box back

6¾ in

4¾ in

4¾ in

4¾ in

4¾ in

hammer frets into slots (p 43). This fret pattern is for a standard chromatic scale as found on all guitars and is based on a 23½ in string length.

8 In stages, tightly secure box and then glue box and fretboard together placing glue on all points of contact.

9 Install tuners and attach strings. Use standard guitar strings of the following gauges: bass string–.022 in wound; middle string–.012 in; and highest string–.010 in.

10 Make a nut and bridge. The strings at the nut should be slightly higher than the first fret. The bridge should be high enough so you can play up and down the scale without strings hitting any obstruction.

11 Tune to standard guitar tuning using octaves, fifths, and fourths. The Puerto Rican Tres is tuned B–G–D.

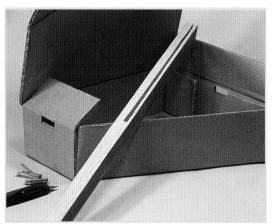

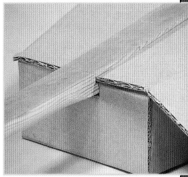

Top left *Sound box ready to receive neck*

Top right *Fitting neck to sound box*

Bottom *Some of neck thickness cut away to create peg head*

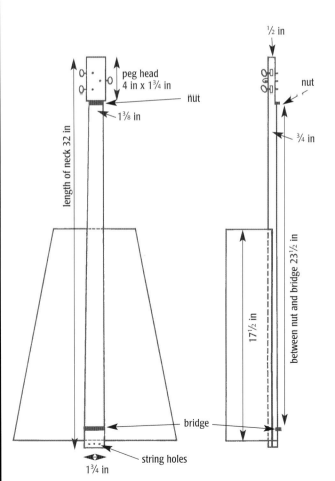

peg head
4 in x 1¾ in

nut

length of neck 32 in

1⅜ in

between nut and bridge 23½ in

17½ in

bridge

string holes

1¾ in

½ in

nut

¾ in

nut

bridge

Fret placement will approximate this configuration.

String length between nut and bridge – 23½ in. Measure from the nut.

1¼ in
2½ in
3⅝ in
4¾ in
5⅞ in
6⅞ in
7¾ in
8⅝ in
9½ in
10¼ in
11 in
11¾ in

4-String Guitar

With four strings, sometimes doubled, the cuatro is found throughout South America and the Caribbean where it is used to accompany singing and dancing. This project has a sound box construction that approximates the more usual hourglass guitar shape.

Materials

2 cardboard cylinders (same or different diameters) for
    sound box body
thin plywood for soundboard and back of sound box
wood stick for neck
wood pieces for nut and bridge
strings
fret wire
machine tuners
hitch pins

Procedure

1 Cut two 4 in segments of cardboard tubing. Use 10½ in diameter material for the lower portion and 9 in diameter material for the upper part, as shown. Mark slots for fitting sections together. Using saw and utility knife, carefully cut out.

2 Cut wood for the neck, as shown. The neck is cut away under the soundboard to allow for freer vibration. Mark and cut a slot into the tube assemblage to receive the neck, as shown (p 50).

3 Using the double tube assemblage as a pattern trace outline onto thin plywood, cut out soundboard and back of instrument (two pieces), as shown. Optionally, a soundhole (3½ to 4 in) may be cut into the back of the instrument.

Top left *Cutting tube to size*

Bottom *Two tube configuration*

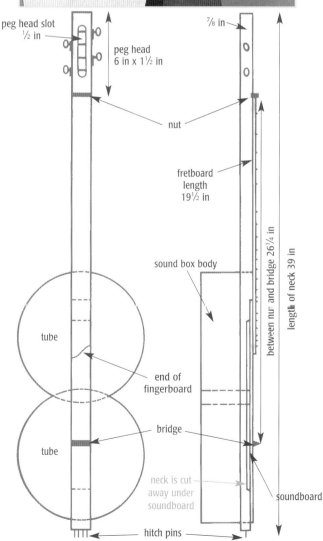

peg head slot
½ in

peg head
6 in x 1½ in

⅞ in

nut

fretboard
length
19½ in

sound box body

between nut and bridge 26¼ in

length of neck 39 in

tube

end of fingerboard

tube

bridge

neck is cut away under soundboard

soundboard

hitch pins

4 Fashion peg head to accommodate tuning mechanisms. See standard slot design (p 42). Round back of neck to shape.

5 For this project, prepare a separate fretboard from thin hardwood stock which will attach to the neck. Determine exact string length (nut to bridge) and set up fretboard to receive frets for a chromatic scale (see p 43 for fretting procedure).

6 Fit all components together without glue and make any adjustments necessary.

7 In stages, glue all parts together: the two cylindrical sound box tubes, neck to sound box, top and back to sound box, fretboard to neck/sound box. Prepare nut and bridge.

Above *Fitting neck to sound box*
Right *Fitting top to sound box*

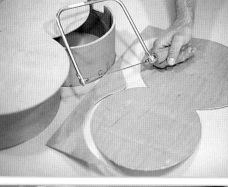

8 Attach tuning mechanisms on peg head and hitch pins in tail end for securing strings. Attach strings using common, lightweight guitar strings.

9 Adjust the string action. The strings at the nut should be slightly higher than the first fret. The bridge should be high enough so you can play up and down the scale without strings bumping into frets farther up the fretboard.

10 Use standard guitar tunings.

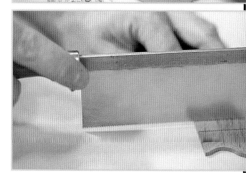

String length between nut and bridge — 26¼ in. Measure from the nut.
1⁷⁄₁₆ in
2⁷⁄₈ in
4⅛ in
5⅜ in
6⁹⁄₁₆ in
7¹¹⁄₁₆ in
8¹¹⁄₁₆ in
9¹¹⁄₁₆ in
10⁹⁄₁₆ in
11⁷⁄₁₆ in
12¼ in
13¹⁄₁₆ in
13¹³⁄₁₆ in
14½ in
15⅛ in
15¾ in
16⅜ in
16⅞ in
17⁷⁄₁₆ in
17¹⁵⁄₁₆ in
18⅜ in
18¹³⁄₁₆ in

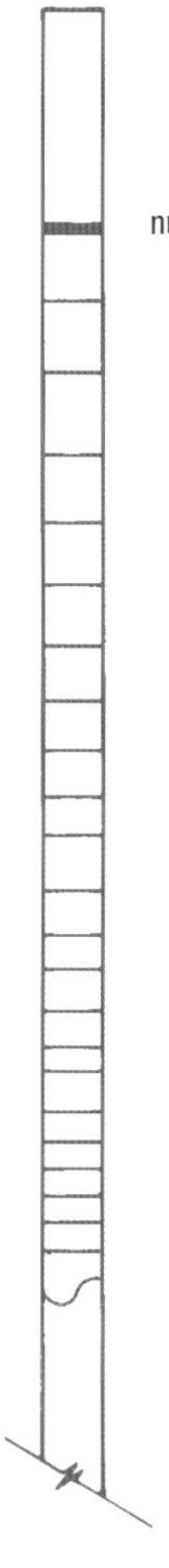

nut

Fret placement will approximate this configuration.

Left *cuatro*   Right *tres*

Above *Cutting fret slots in fretboard and drilling holes for hitch pins*

5-String Folk Banjo

With roots in Africa, the banjo developed in interesting ways in the United States and spawned several variant forms. This project is based on an ol' time five-string Appalachian banjo design that features a shortened fifth string used as a rhythmic element as well as a type of drone. The round construction of the banjo sound box is easily accommodated with large diameter cardboard tubing. Making the neck of this project is more challenging.

Materials

cardboard cylinder for sound box
thin plywood for soundboard
2x4 wood for neck
⅛ in hardwood stock for fretboard
wood pieces for nut and bridge
standard lightweight banjo strings
fret wire
machine tuners

Procedure

1 For sound box or "pot" use a segment of thick-walled, 9 in diameter cardboard tubing. The depth of the pot is variable so long as it accommodates the neck.

2 Transfer all the measurements for the neck to the neck stock (see diagram, p 52). Draw the top view and the side view onto the wood (see below). Double check all lines and measurements. It may be easier to draw an actual-size pattern of the neck on paper and then trace it onto the wood. Make sure the fifth peg is on the proper side. Some left-handed players place it on the other side.

3 Before you cut out the neck, think through the process carefully. Saw the neck one area at a time. The peg head shape must be reconciled with tuning mechanisms.

4 With a file and sandpaper, begin shaping the back of the neck and smoothing all surfaces. Study other banjo necks to get the right shape.

5 Cut a notch in the pot, as shown, to receive the neck. Mark, saw, and fit carefully.

Fitting neck and soundboard to banjo pot

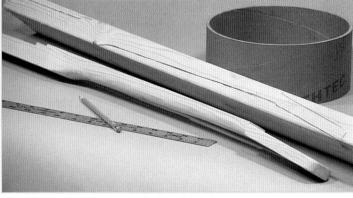

Marking neck pattern onto 2x4 neck blank

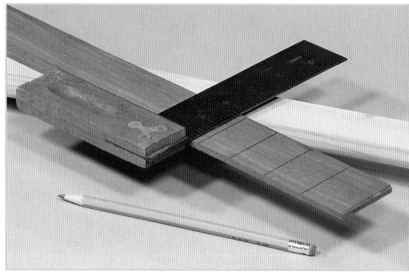

6 Place the pot assembly onto ⅛-in-plywood soundboard stock and outline with a pencil. Cut out the design being careful not to chip the plywood.

7 While the ⅛ in thick fretboard stock is still in its rectangular form, starting from the position of the nut, mark the placement of all the frets, as shown, based on a string length of 23⅝ in. Longer and shorter scale lengths may be used but new fret measurements will have to be copied from another instrument or calculated using the *Rule of Eighteen* (p 43).

8 Saw fret slots. Before hammering in frets, trace the outline of the actual neck onto the back of the fretboard and cut out the fretboard. It is most common to glue the fretboard to the neck without frets and install the frets afterwards. As you prepare to glue the fretboard to the neck, it is important that the relationship (measurements) between the nut, frets, and bridge be maintained in order for the instrument to play in tune.

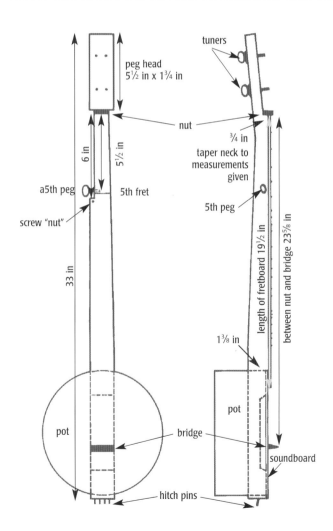

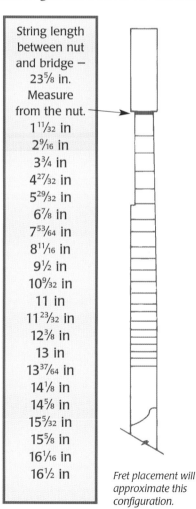

String length between nut and bridge – 23⅝ in. Measure from the nut.
1¹¹/₃₂ in
2⁹/₁₆ in
3¾ in
4²⁷/₃₂ in
5²⁹/₃₂ in
6⅞ in
7⁵³/₆₄ in
8¹¹/₁₆ in
9½ in
10⁹/₃₂ in
11 in
11²³/₃₂ in
12⅜ in
13 in
13³⁷/₆₄ in
14⅛ in
14⅝ in
15⁵/₃₂ in
15⅝ in
16¹/₁₆ in
16½ in

Fret placement will approximate this configuration.

Top *Preparing neck, fretboard, and peg head*
Middle *Tailpiece components*
Bottom *Fifth peg arrangement*

9 Carefully position machine tuners on the back of the peg head and mark the point at which each tuner post will pass through the peg head. Drill the holes through the back of the peg head.

10 The fifth peg will be installed into the side of the neck just behind the fifth fret, 5½ in from the nut. This requires drilling a hole at this position. Since there are slight differences between styles of fifth pegs, measure the one you have purchased and proceed accordingly.

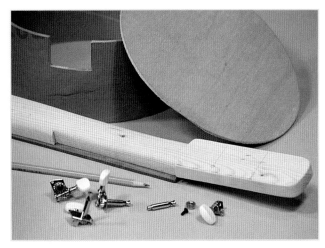

11 After making any final adjustments, glue the parts together in sequence: neck to pot, top to pot, and fingerboard to neck.

12 Bone, hardened plastic, or any very hard wood such as ebony may be used for the nut. Shape and glue in place at the end of the fingerboard. With a fine saw blade or knife-file, cut four equidistant slots into the nut. To insure against unwanted string buzzes, cut the slots at a slight angle so they will slope from the tuners and pass out of the nut slot just barely (¹⁄₃₂ in) above the fingerboard and first fret.

13 The height and width of the bridge are a matter of personal preference. Usually, the height of the bridge will be between ⅜ to ½ in and about 2 to 2½ in long. It is easiest to purchase a ready-made banjo bridge.

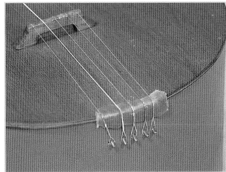

14 Five small pins for anchoring the strings at the tail end of the banjo are now positioned, pre-drilled, and hammered in. Use small finishing nails or buy piano bridge pins or zither hitch pins from your local music store.

15 Hammer the fifth peg into the side of the neck. Attach a small slot-head screw immediately in front of the fifth peg. This acts as a tiny nut and guides the fifth string along the appropriate trajectory to the bridge, as shown.

16 Place the tuners on the peg head, pre-drill screw holes, and attach securely with appropriate screws.

17 Light- or medium-gauge, loop-end strings work well and can be purchased in sets made especially for banjo at most music stores. Use a small piece of leather or other resilient material to protect the area where the strings pass from hitch pins up-and-over the edge of the pot so strings will not cut into wood. Tension strings and add bridge.

18 Try the following common banjo tuning.

String
5th—E (highest note)
4th—B (lowest note)
3rd—E (one octave lower than 5th string)
2nd—G#
1st—B

19 To learn to play the banjo take a lesson or two from an experienced teacher or refer to an instruction book.

Mando-Banjo

Reminiscent of designs popular in the early 1900s, this instrument is a combination of mandolin and tenor banjos, instruments that came in a variety of sizes during that jazz-crazed period. This instrument project is based on actual modern mandolin measurements.

Materials

cardboard cylinder for sound box pot
thin plywood for soundboard
1x2 wood for neck
wood pieces for bridge and nut
strings
fret wire
machine tuners

Procedure

1 Use a segment of thick-walled, 12-in-diameter cardboard tubing for sound box. The actual depth is variable so long as it accommodates the neck.

2 Transfer all measurements from neck diagram onto the neck stock. Draw the top view and the side view onto the wood. Optionally, a slight taper on the sides of the neck going from sound box to nut adds a neater look. Prepare peg head configuration (p 42). Cut out neck and peg head. File and sand.

3 Using the neck as a template, plot placement of the notches in the cardboard tube. Mark, saw, and cut notches in the sound box, as shown, to receive the neck. Fit carefully.

4 The string length for the mando-banjo is 13⁷⁄₈ in. On the neck (or separate fingerboard, if

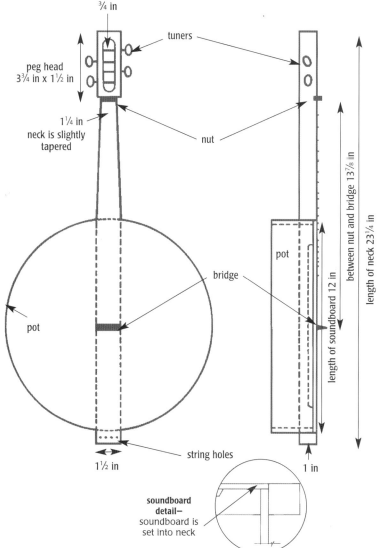

peg head
3³⁄₄ in x 1¹⁄₂ in

¾ in

tuners

1¼ in
neck is slightly tapered

nut

length of neck 23¹⁄₄ in

between nut and bridge 13⁷⁄₈ in

pot

bridge

pot

length of soundboard 12 in

string holes

1½ in

1 in

soundboard detail—
soundboard is set into neck

Cutting notch for neck

you wish), determine the position of the nut and cut a slot for it. From the nut, clearly and precisely mark the placement of all the frets, as shown. Longer and shorter scale lengths may be used but new fret measurements will have to be copied from another instrument or calculated using the *Rule of Eighteen* (p 43).

5   Saw fret slots. It is important that the measurements between the nut, frets, and bridge be maintained in order for the instrument to play in tune. Install and finish frets (p 43).

6   Using file and sandpaper, continue to shape the back of the neck and smooth all surfaces.

7   Carefully position the machine head tuners and mark the point at which each tuner post passes into the peg head slot. Using a drill bit slightly larger than the tuner post (usually ¼ in), drill the holes.

8   Place the assembly onto ⅛-in-plywood stock to be used for the top and outline with a pencil. Cut out the design being careful not to chip the plywood.

9   Assemble all the parts without glue and make adjustments. Fit the soundboard/neck junction carefully for a neat look. Then glue the parts together in sequence: neck to sound box, soundboard top to sound box.

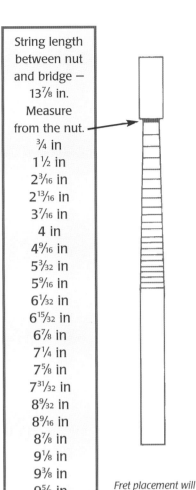

String length between nut and bridge — 13⅞ in. Measure from the nut.
¾ in
1½ in
2³⁄₁₆ in
2¹³⁄₁₆ in
3⁷⁄₁₆ in
4 in
4⁹⁄₁₆ in
5³⁄₃₂ in
5⁹⁄₁₆ in
6¹⁄₃₂ in
6¹⁵⁄₃₂ in
6⅞ in
7¼ in
7⅝ in
7³¹⁄₃₂ in
8⁹⁄₃₂ in
8⁹⁄₁₆ in
8⅞ in
9⅛ in
9⅜ in
9⅝ in

Fret placement will approximate this configuration.

10   Cut a nut. Shape and glue in place. With a fine saw blade or knife-file, cut four equidistant slots into the nut to just barely above the fingerboard and first fret.

11   Design and make a bridge to accommodate the four strings. Bridge should be approximately ¼ in high and 2½ in long. Cut fine shallow slots into the bridge for each string.

12   Now drill four small holes for anchoring the strings at the tail end of the mando-banjo. Small hitch pins may serve a similar purpose.

13   Place the tuners on the peg head, pre-drill small holes, and attach securely with appropriate screws.

14   Light-gauge mandolin strings work well and are found in ready-made sets at most music stores. Since mandolin strings come in sets of eight (each string is doubled), you will need only half the set.

15   Tension strings and add bridge. Adjust the string action. Strings at the nut should be slightly higher than the first fret. The bridge should be high enough so you can play up and down the scale without strings bumping into frets farther up the fingerboard.

16   Tune strings to G–D–A–E (low to high). Several tunings are usually necessary before the instrument stabilizes. Find a book or musician to help in final adjustments.

Top *Cutting neck to accommodate soundboard*

Upper middle *Tailpiece and bridge*

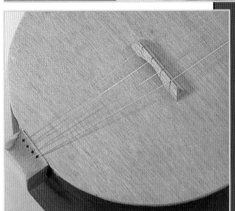

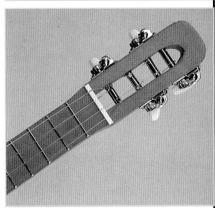

Lower middle *Neck/soundboard/pot juncture*

Bottom *Tuners, peg head, and nut*

Fiddles

Folk Fiddle

The Appalachian Mountain fiddle or devil's box has taken its place among the most important instruments in American folklore heritage. Some of the earliest homemade fiddles were constructed from cigar boxes, kitchen tins, and other utility items.

Materials

flat cardboard for sound box body
2x4 wood for neck and fingerboard
wood piece for nut and an optional violin
    bridge
lightweight violin strings
machine tuners or violin pegs
violin bow

Procedure

1 Plot the basic pattern measurements for sound box body on flat cardboard and cut out. (Pattern is same for dulcitar, p 45.)

2 Incise, crimp, and fold (p 41) into box shape. Make adjustments.

3 Transfer measurements for fiddle neck to wood stock and carefully cut out. Drill holes for your chosen tuners. If you wish

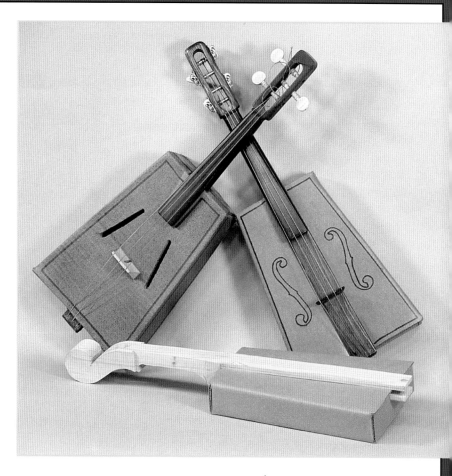

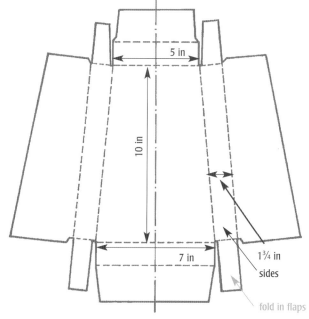

5 in

10 in

7 in

1¾ in
sides

fold in flaps

Sound box pattern cut and folded, and neck with slot for attaching neck to sound box

to design a more elaborate violin-like peg head, decide on tuning devices (machine heads or friction pegs) and draw your design on paper then trace directly onto wood stock (see photo p 58). Take time to think the process through. File and sand neck and peg head.

4 Fit neck to sound box. The neck is slotted or "clothespinned" onto the sound box hiding the front seam (see dulcitar, p 45, and bottom photograph, below). Make whatever modification may be necessary to achieve a good fit between these components.

5 In order to achieve the appropriate string trajectory, shape a tapered fingerboard, as shown, and attach to the neck. Round fingerboard slightly and smooth out imperfections.

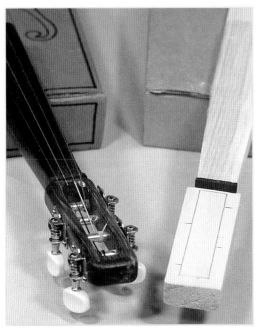

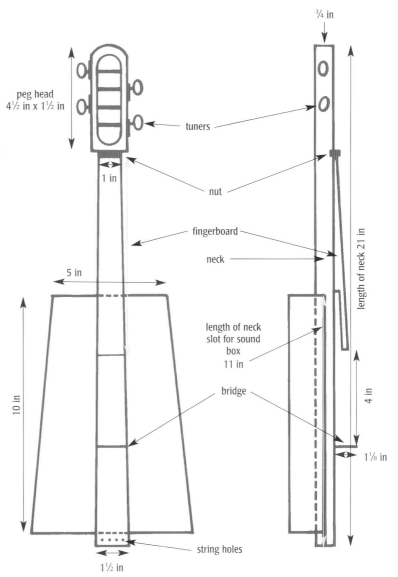

peg head
4½ in x 1½ in

1 in

tuners

nut

fingerboard

neck

5 in

10 in

string holes

1½ in

¾ in

length of neck 21 in

length of neck slot for sound box
11 in

bridge

4 in

1⅛ in

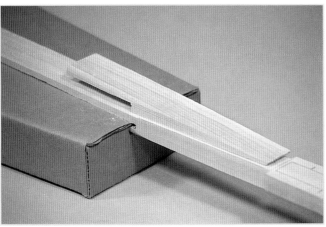

Fingerboard placed on neck

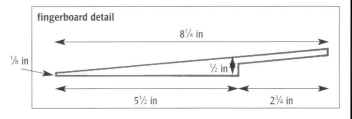

fingerboard detail

8¼ in

⅛ in

½ in

5½ in

2¾ in

6 Mark and drill holes at tail end of instrument to secure strings.

7 Make nut of hardwood or other brittle material. Cut four equidistant shallow grooves in the nut to seat the strings. Strings are very close but not touching the fingerboard at the nut.

8 Purchase a violin bridge or make your own simplified version. The bridge should be as high as necessary for the strings to slightly incline above the fingerboard as they pass from nut to bridge.

9 Install tuning mechanisms.

10 Attach lightweight violin strings in their traditional arrangement.

11 Bring strings up in pitch. A beginning violin book or your local fiddler will help you get started. The following tuning is standard violin tuning.

G (lowest string)

D

A

E (highest string)

12 Purchase an inexpensive violin bow at your local music store. Don't forget the rosin!

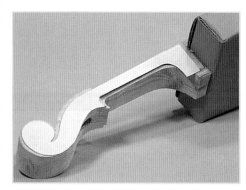

The more elaborate scroll design for neck requires a modified junction at sound box.

Chinese Fiddl

The unique feature of this two-string family of fiddles is that the bow hair is twined between the two strings thus making it inseparable from the body and neck of the instrument. By using an underhand bow grip and pushing the bow out and in, relative to the neck, each string can be sounded individually. The lyrical singing quality of this instrument, the erhu, is typical of traditional Chinese music.

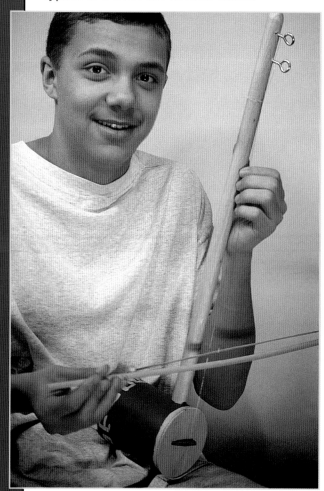

Materials
cardboard tubing for sound box body
⅛ in plywood for soundboard
wood dowel or broom stick for neck
2 screw eyes or machine tuners
thin music wire
a length of thin flexible stick and unwaxed
    dental floss for the bow and rosin

Procedure

1 Cut 26 in of ⅞ in doweling for the neck and drill a small hole (or add a hitch pin) at the tail end for securing the strings.

2 Cut a 4½ in segment of 3¾-in-diameter cardboard tubing and drill a ⅞ in hole through the tube to receive the neck. See diagram for placement.

3 Spike the length of doweling through the tube. Attach screw eyes or appropriate tuners in line with each other at the peg head end of the dowel.

4 Cut a soundboard of ⅛ in plywood or 2-ply cardboard the same diameter as the tube and glue it to the end closest to the neck.

5 The bow should be made at this stage since the bow hair goes between the two strings. Cut a 2 ft length of thin flexible doweling (¼ to 5⁄16 in) and make a hole or slot in each end for securing the bow hair, as shown. Although most bows use horse hair, in this case, several strands of unwaxed dental floss amply coated with violin rosin will suffice. Tie and secure strands of dental floss under as much tension as possible without breaking the stick. Small pieces of wood (⅜ in doweling) can be inserted under the bow hair, as shown, for increased tension. Rosin bow hair liberally and often.

6 Tie lower-pitched music string (.010 in) between tail and far tuner. Higher-pitched string (also .010 in) must pass between bow stick and bow hair, then be secured to other tuner.

7 A nylon string noose, which will act as a nut, is now tied around the neck and strings about 3 in from the nearest tuner thus defining a specific string length for both strings. Positioning of the noose-nut is variable but this project measures the distance between bridge and nut at about 17 in.

8 Traditionally, strings are tuned to the interval of a musical fifth. Hold instrument, as shown. Higher string is usually activated by pressing in on the bow. Lower string is played by lifting bow.

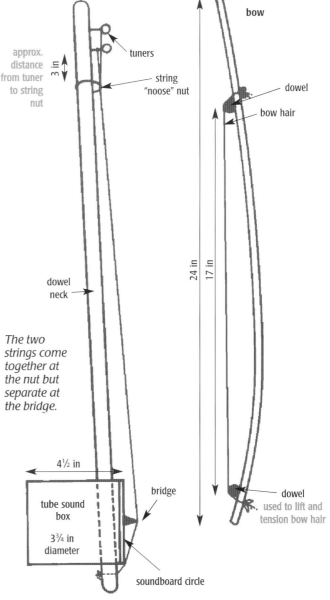

approx. distance from tuner to string nut

3 in

tuners

string "noose" nut

bow

dowel

bow hair

dowel neck

24 in

17 in

The two strings come together at the nut but separate at the bridge.

4½ in

tube sound box

3¾ in diameter

bridge

dowel used to lift and tension bow hair

soundboard circle

Zithers

Appalachian Zither

The Appalachian dulcimer is a popular traditional instrument of the southeastern United States. European in origin, the instrument comes in many shapes: hourglass, teardrop, boat, and elongated diamond. Since cardboard does not readily bend into curved shapes, this project uses the basic trapezoid shape. The diatonic fret arrangement makes this an easy instrument to play.

Materials

flat cardboard for sound box body
wood stick for fretboard
wood pieces for nut and bridge
strings
fret wire
machine tuners

Procedure

1 Plot the basic pattern measurements for sound box body (p 61) on flat cardboard and cut out.
2 Incise, crimp, and fold (p 41) into box shape. Design and cut soundholes, as desired. Make adjustments.

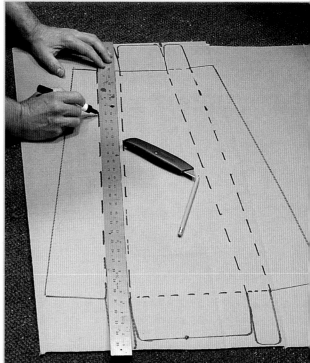

Transferring pattern to cardboard

3　Measure the fretboard 31 in x 1⅜ In x ¾ In and mark according to diagram (p63).

4　Draw the peg head slot onto the fretboard (p 42). Sand the entire fretboard flat and smooth. Using a rasp file or other tool, fashion an optional 4-in-long strum hollow about ⅛ in deep, as shown.

5　The scale length (distance between nut and bridge) is 25¾ in. Measure and mark the position of the nut and bridge. The nut should be just in front of the peg slot and the bridge just beyond the strum hollow. Make the nut and bridge from bone, hardwood, or hard plastic. Cut a slot across the fingerboard with an appropriate saw to hold the nut. It should fit snugly into the slot. You can make a slot for the bridge but it is sometimes advisable to have a floating bridge that can be adjusted after stringing the instrument to correct any intonation difficulties.

6　Using a small square, measure and mark the fret positions, as shown. Each calibration is measured from the nut. Mark as accurately as possible.

Note　Find your own fret placements for other scale lengths by using the *Rule of Eighteen* (p 43) which will

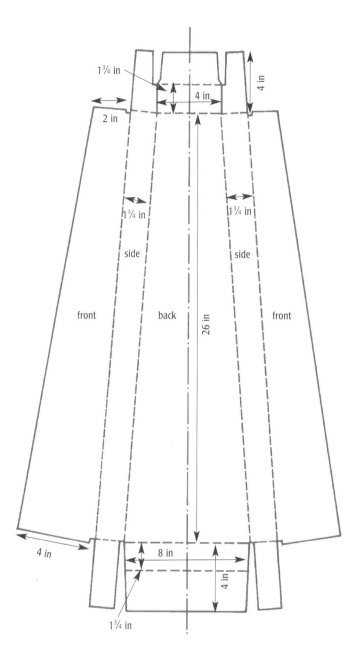

Cutting, crimping, and folding sound box

Top *Cutting fret slots and strum hollow*

Upper middle *Inserting frets*

result in a chromatic scale (all semitones). Leave out the chromatic frets 1, 3, 6, 8, 11, 13, 15, 18, 20, 23, 25, and 27 for a diatonic (regular do-re-mi . . .) scale, appropriate for the dulcimer.

7   Carefully cut fret slots (p 43).

8   Insert frets firmly into the fret slots. Leave frets slightly longer than the width of the fingerboard and clip and file off the excess after they are all in place. Round the top ends of each fret using a fine metal file or fine sandpaper to remove sharp tips that might nick fingers.

9   Drill pegholes into the peg head to match the tuners you choose. A three-string dulcimer is more traditional and a little easier to play. A four-string dulcimer is usually arranged with a double course melody string that adds a bit more tone. If you want to make a four-string instrument, simply make the necessary adjustments for the extra tuner and string. Do not attach the tuners at this stage.

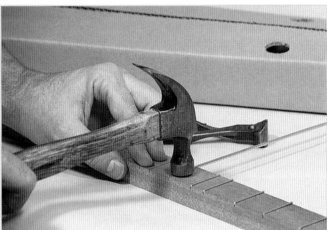

10   Place the fretboard directly down the center of the top soundboard piece, double check all measurements, and glue firmly into place.

11   Put tuners onto the peg head and fasten (p 63).

12   Small finishing nails or other material will suffice for hitch pins. Hammer pins in the end of the fingerboard leaving about ¼ in protruding (p 63).

13   Mark the string spacings on the top edges of the nut and bridge. With a fine saw or file, cut shallow slots at a slight angle on the nut to about ¹⁄₃₂ in above the surface of the fretboard. For the bridge, slightly angled slots are cut to within ³⁄₁₆ in from the surface of the fretboard.

14   Use banjo or guitar strings with these string gauges:
    Bass string − .022 in wound with nickel or brass winding
    Melody string and middle string − .010 or .012 in plain strings.

15   For easy playing, make final adjustments to the instrument's string action. The strings should pass as close to the first fret as possible without buzzing. To adjust the bridge height, the strings must pass as close as possible to every fret without buzzing as you play up the scale.

Lower middle *Drilling tuning peg holes*

Bottom *Filing frets in preparation to glue neck to sound box*

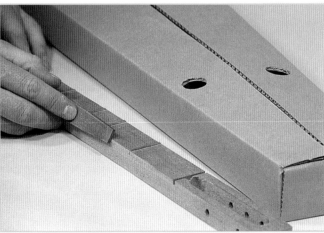

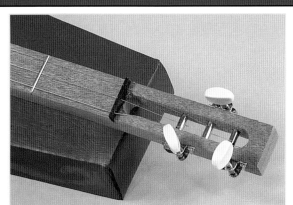

Top *Nut and tuners*
Bottom *Strum hollow bridge and tailpiece*

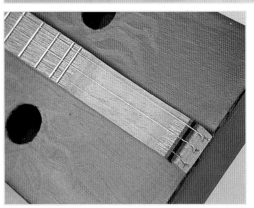

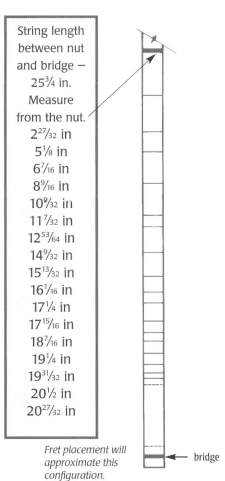

String length
between nut
and bridge –
25³/₄ in.
Measure
from the nut.
2²⁷/₃₂ in
5¹/₈ in
6⁷/₁₆ in
8⁹/₁₆ in
10⁹/₃₂ in
11⁷/₃₂ in
12⁵³/₆₄ in
14⁹/₃₂ in
15¹³/₃₂ in
16¹/₁₆ in
17¹/₄ in
17¹⁵/₁₆ in
18⁷/₁₆ in
19¹/₄ in
19³¹/₃₂ in
20¹/₂ in
20²⁷/₃₂ in

*Fret placement will
approximate this
configuration.*

← bridge

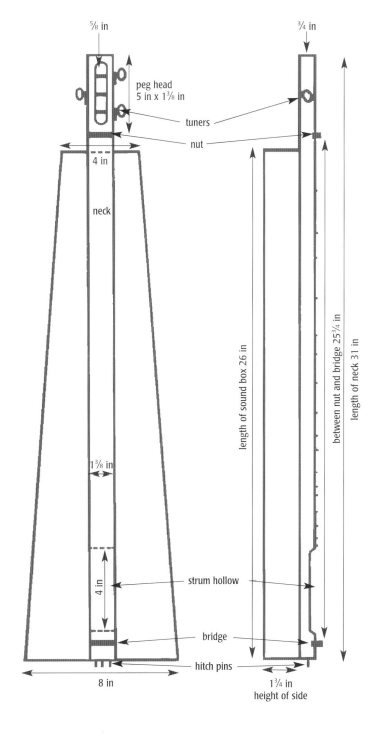

⁵/₈ in

³/₄ in

peg head
5 in x 1³/₈ in

tuners

nut

4 in

neck

1³/₈ in

length of sound box 26 in

between nut and bridge 25³/₄ in

length of neck 31 in

4 in

strum hollow

bridge

hitch pins

8 in

1³/₄ in
height of side

Japanese Zither

Most likely of ancient historical Chinese origin, the koto has become a musical symbol of Japanese culture. Contemporary versions of this instrument are quite large with thirteen silk strings and movable bridges. This koto project is based on the earlier, smaller, Chinese long zither called zheng which uses thin metal strings instead of silk.

Materials

flat cardboard for sound box body
2 hardwood pieces for end blocks
wood for bridges
zither pins and hitch pins
thin metal music wire

Procedure

1 Plot the basic pattern measurements on a flat piece of double thickness cardboard. (Although the body is usually tapered, an easier option is to make it rectangular, as we did with the Asian zither in Part 1, p 22).

2 Cut out the design, incise along the fold lines, crimp for easy folding, and fold into shape (p 41). Make any necessary adjustments.

3 Measure and fit hardwood end blocks to both ends of the instrument body. Wood braces may also be glued to the inside of the playing surface, as shown, for extra stability.

4 Once end block components are carefully fitted to the ends of the sound box, glue them in place and fold and secure the entire box enclosure around the end blocks.

5 Cut a series of wood bridges approximately 2 in high, as shown on p 65. The bridges remain movable for fine tuning and are not glued to the instrument.

6 Cut strips of wood to act as the end nuts and glue to the surface at each end to keep the strings from cutting into the cardboard as the strings go to the tuning pins and hitch pins.

7 Position zither pins equidistant along the wider end and hitch pins across the opposite end. Before drilling zither pin holes in the end block, test on a scrap of wood to insure a tight fit for the pins since they will have to hold strings under tension.

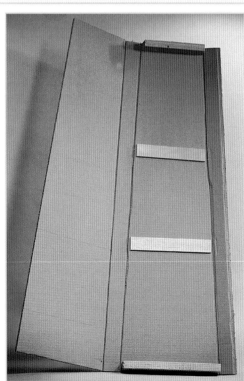

End blocks and braces glued in place

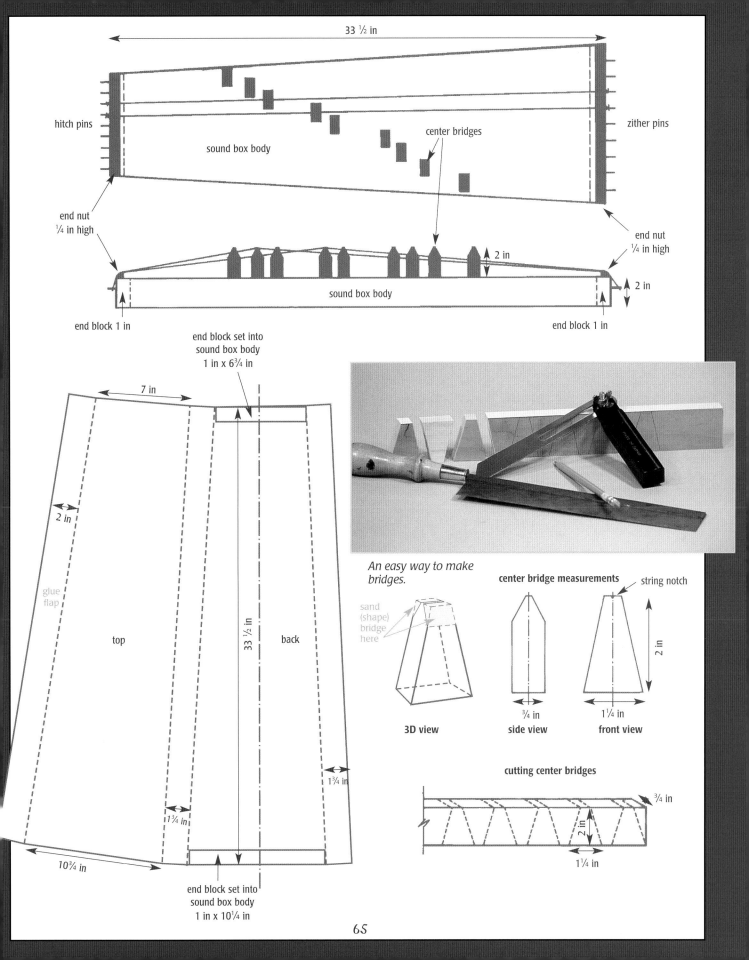

33 ½ in

hitch pins

sound box body

zither pins

center bridges

end nut
¼ in high

end nut
¼ in high

2 in

sound box body

2 in

end block 1 in

end block 1 in

end block set into
sound box body
1 in x 6¾ in

7 in

2 in

glue
flap

top

33 ½ in

back

1¾ in

1¾ in

10¾ in

end block set into
sound box body
1 in x 10¼ in

*An easy way to make
bridges.*

center bridge measurements

string notch

sand
(shape)
bridge
here

2 in

¾ in

1¼ in

3D view

side view

front view

cutting center bridges

¾ in

2 in

1¼ in

8 After securing zither pins and hitch pins in place, begin the stringing process. One or two gauges of relatively thin string (.010 and .012) should be sufficient with the thicker string for the three or four lowest sounding string courses.

9 Asian zithers are tuned to a pentatonic scale. Place bridges in roughly the same pattern, as shown in diagram. Tighten the lowest string to the degree where it begins to sound a clear pitch. Tune the pentatonic scale to the 1−2−3−5−6 scale degrees of a regular scale. A musician can help you if need be. Some experimentation may be necessary to find the point at which all strings sound best. Note that a correlation between string tension and bridge placement will help bring the scale into conformation.

10 To play, strings are plucked with the fingertips at the wide end. Characteristic ornamentation is achieved by depressing a sounding string with the other hand on the opposite side of the bridge producing a sliding or portamento effect.

Preparing bridges and end nut. Shape (sand) front and back of each bridge, as shown in drawing (p 65), to create a more definite point of contact for the string and greatly enhance tonal quality.

Plucking string on one end and pushing on it on the opposite side of the bridge produces a sliding pitch change.

East Indian Zither

The East Indian zither (veena) is found predominately in the south of India and is a close relative to the more popular North Indian sitar. The veena is characterized by movable frets and a unique playing style. This project uses cardboard tubing instead of bamboo for the neck and sections of construction tube for resonators instead of the traditional gourds.

Materials

3½-in-diameter cardboard tubing for neck
10-in-diameter construction tubing for resonators
⅛ in plywood for soundboard
wood pieces for end blocks
other wood for neck cradles
quarter-round molding for fret rails
large nails for frets
nuts and bolts
rubber bands or cord for tying on frets
hitch pins
strings

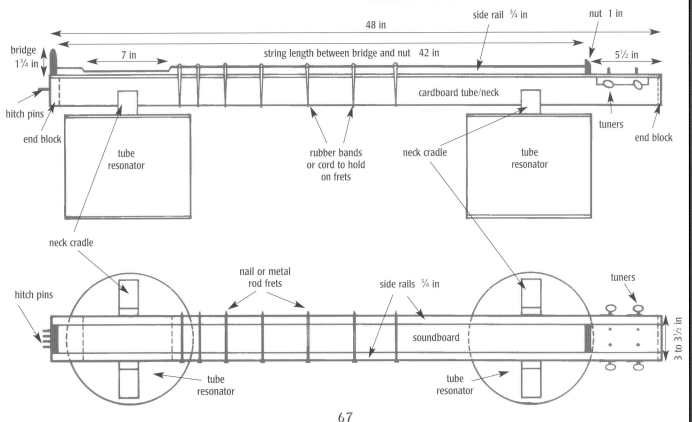

48 in

side rail ¾ in

nut 1 in

string length between bridge and nut 42 in

bridge 1¾ in

7 in

5½ in

cardboard tube/neck

hitch pins

end block

tube resonator

rubber bands or cord to hold on frets

neck cradle

tube resonator

tuners

end block

neck cradle

nail or metal rod frets

side rails ¾ in

tuners

hitch pins

soundboard

3 to 3½ in

tube resonator

tube resonator

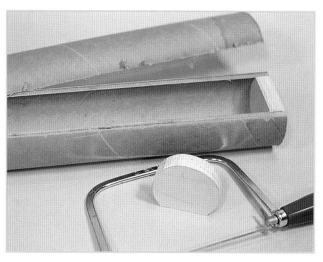

Cutting tube and fitting end block

Procedure

1 Use a sturdy 3½-in-diameter cardboard tube 48 in long for neck of the instrument. Cut the tube lengthwise so that about two-thirds of the tube remains, as shown.

2 Using the tube as a guide, cut hardwood end blocks to fit snugly inside each end of the tube. Glue into place. Cut notches into the peg head end to accommodate the tuning peg arrangement, as shown.

3 Cut two 8 in sections of 10-in-diameter construction tubing for resonators (available at most home centers).

4 Enclose top end of each resonator with ⅛ in plywood. For increased acoustic effect, cut holes into the plywood pieces that cover the bottom ends of each resonator, as shown.

5 Now cut wood pieces, as shown, to cradle and stabilize the joining of the neck to the resonators. Glue the wood cradles to each resonator. Attach each resonator to the neck by drilling a hole through each assemblage and bolting them together, as shown.

6 For the soundboard, cut a length of ⅛ in plywood that will cover the open area of the neck tube. At the peg head end glue a block of ½ in thick wood to the inside of the soundboard which will hold the tuners and nest into the notches previously cut for this purpose. See photograph to attach tuners to the peg head. Carefully measure, fit, and drill holes for the tuners. Secure tuners with screws.

7 Now glue soundboard/peg head assemblage to the neck.

8 Glue two strips of ¾ in quarter-round trim to the outer edges of the soundboard leaving space to accommodate the nut and bridge at the ends.

9 Cut pieces of wood for nut and bridge. Nut is about 1 in high and the bridge

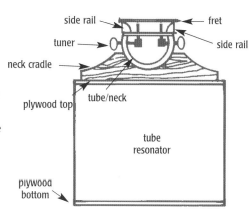

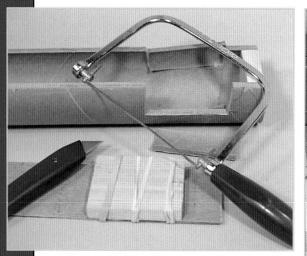

Above *Preparing peg head area*
Middle *Gluing top and bottom on resonators*
Right *Attaching neck to resonator*

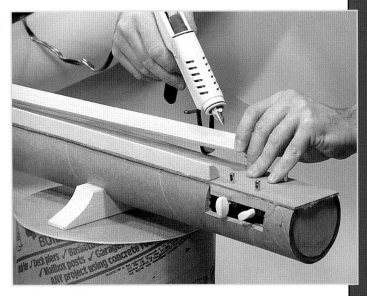

Gluing side rails to soundboard

is about 1¾ in high. Glue into place.

10 Find custom length wire (brass has a warmer sound) of diminishing gauges (.020 − .018 − .016 − .014). Purchase at a piano supply store since guitar wire does not usually come in this length. Hammered dulcimer or harpsichord wire is best.

11 Use good-size finishing nails or thin metal rods for frets and sturdy rubber bands (or cord) to secure them and attach, as shown. Space logically. Do not worry about exact placement until strings are attached.

12 Hammer in hitch pins. Attach strings between hitch pins and tuners and tighten so they sound appropriately. Use a combination of octaves, fourths, and fifths between strings.

13 Now move the frets so they make a musical scale or mode. Note In India, modes are called ragas. There are many forms of ragas each having its own sophisticated symbolic meanings and performance mandates. For this instrument project, begin with a standard diatonic do-re-mi scale and explore more exotic scales when you're ready.

Attaching frets

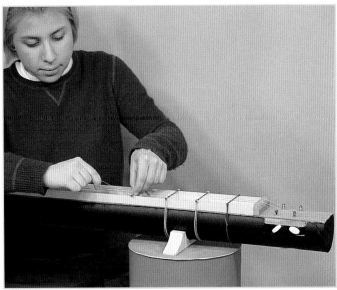

Harps and Lyres

Irish Harp

The Irish or Celtic harp (clarsach) was used to maintain the folklore heritage of the Irish people. A common style is the basic triangular construction between the sound box, neck, and pillar. This project is much simplified from professionally made harps but is true in principle to all harps of this type. Some of the joinery required for this instrument is more challenging than in previous projects.

Materials

flat cardboard for sound box body
1½ in x ¾ in hardwood strip for harp framework
zither pins
strings

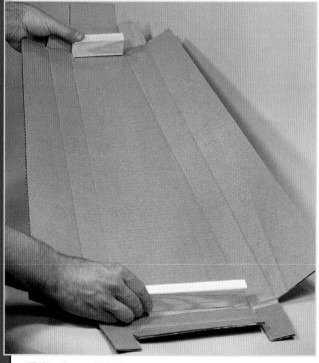

Fitting the end blocks

Procedure

1 Using pattern on p 71, plot the measurements on flat cardboard to make the sound box body. Follow general guidelines provided for the Appalachian zither (p 60).

2 Cut and fold harp box into the desired configuration. Make two end blocks to fit snugly inside the ends of the sound box, as shown. Glue sound box together and let dry.

3 See diagram on p 72 to prepare the harp wood frame. Cut and fit pieces until they form a sturdy unit. Note that the string rib will glue flat (not on its edge) to the sound box. The neck and pillar are notched and fitted on edge to the right side (relative to player) of string rib so that the strings will line up appropriately between the neck and string rib. The lap joint between the neck and pillar requires careful measuring, sawing, and fitting. Adjust as you go until everything fits properly. Don't glue the frame together at this time.

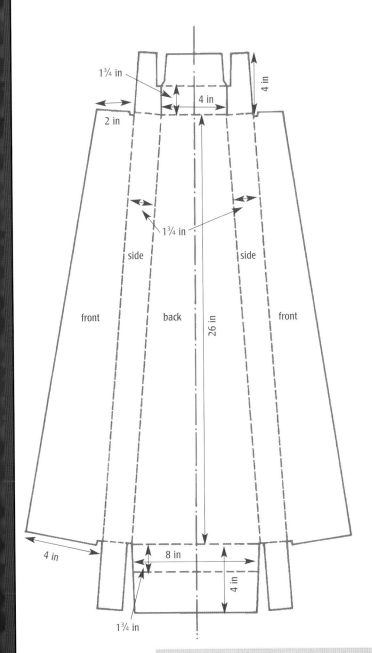

1¾ in

4 in

4 in

2 in

1¾ in

side

side

front

back

front

26 in

4 in

8 in

4 in

1¾ in

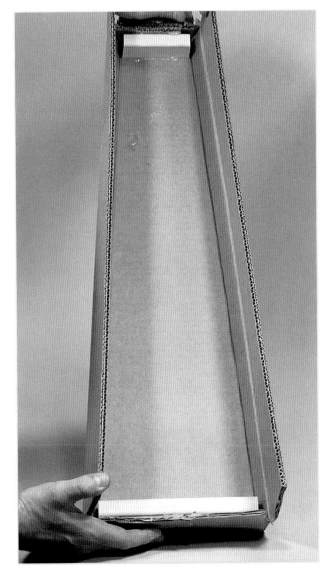

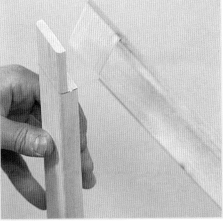

Top right *Sound box partially assembled with end blocks in place.*

Bottom left *Lap joint at neck/pillar junction.*

Bottom right *Harp framework. Note how parts fit together at the joints.*

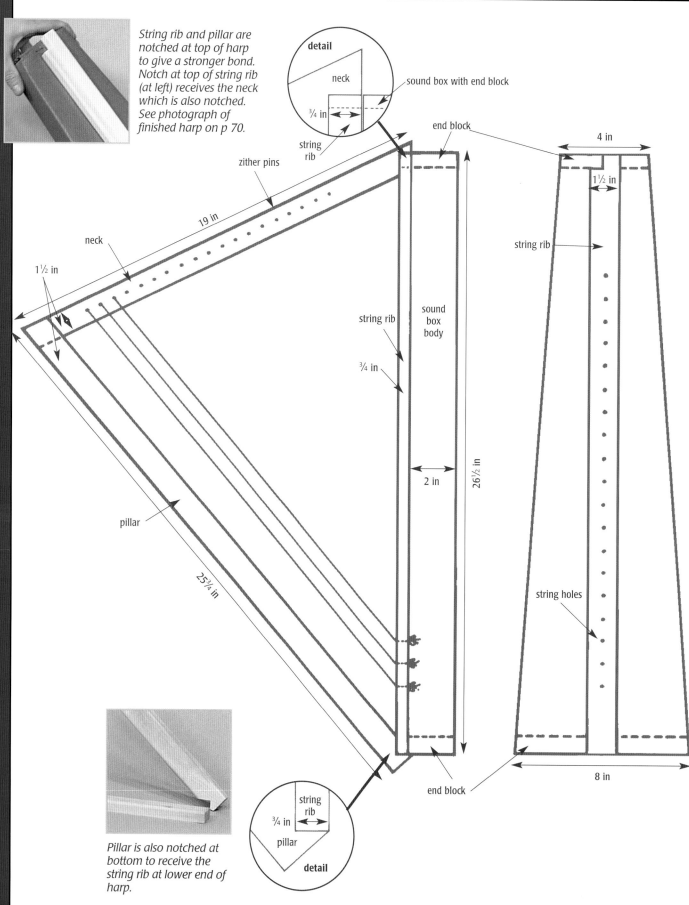

String rib and pillar are notched at top of harp to give a stronger bond. Notch at top of string rib (at left) receives the neck which is also notched. See photograph of finished harp on p 70.

detail

neck

¾ in

string rib

sound box with end block

end block

4 in

1½ in

string rib

zither pins

19 in

neck

1½ in

string rib

sound box body

¾ in

26½ in

2 in

pillar

25¾ in

string rib

¾ in

string holes

end block

8 in

string rib

¾ in

pillar

detail

Pillar is also notched at bottom to receive the string rib at lower end of harp.

4 Decide on the number of strings. Optimally, there should be ½ to ¾ in distance between strings through the area where the fingers will pluck the strings. Spacing is about 1 to 1¼ in along the string rib and about ¾ in along the neck. It is best to make a full-scale drawing first on paper to insure appropriate string spacings. Mark string holes along the string rib.

5 Now glue string rib to the sound box. You may wish to paint the box before gluing on string rib. Make sure there is good contact between string rib and sound box along the full length.

6 Cut access holes in the back of the box, as shown below.

7 Drill small string holes along the string rib and into the sound box.

8 On the neck, mark and drill holes for zither pins. Fit and glue neck to pillar and then glue this combination to the string rib/sound box assemblage.

9 Attach zither pins along the neck of the harp and begin stringing by tying large knots into one end of string (or use toggles) to keep the strings from pulling through the string rib, and thread string from interior of harp through string rib hole and onto its respective tuning pin. Use a variety of fishing line gauges and lightweight weed trimmer string. Experiment and use your own judgment as to what makes good sound and what the instrument will bear. Be aware that the combined pull of all the strings can be quite substantial.

10 Tune to a diatonic scale and hold, as shown on p 70.

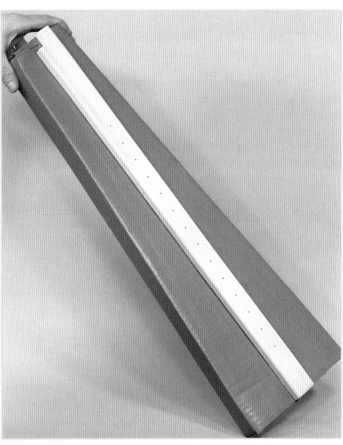

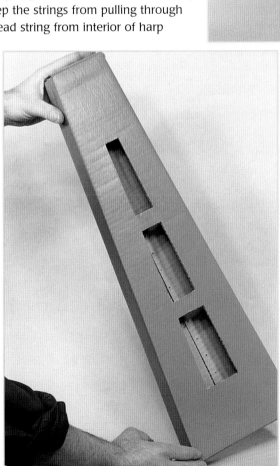

Access holes cut in back of sound box

Top *String rib glued onto sound box*
Bottom *Measure and drill zither pin holes.*

African Harp

This project is a more complex model of the African harp described on p 27. The kora is a primary instrument of the griot, the traditional musical culture bearers of West Africa. Using the kora for accompaniment, griot are the carriers of news and are essential for all important occasions such as births, succession, and funerals. The traditional kora has twenty-one strings. In this project a truncated box takes the place of the huge calabash usually used for the sound chamber.

Materials

flat cardboard for sound box body
2 large dowels for handles
one long flat stick for neck
zither pins
variety of nylon strings

Procedure

1 Plot the pattern measurements (p 76) onto a piece of flat cardboard and cut out. Incise, crimp, and fold (p 41) into shape.

2 The placement of the neck (¾ in x 1¼ in x 38 in) and the two dowel handles (1 in x 24 in) on either side of the neck should be marked onto the box. See diagram on p 75. The dowels need to be long enough to go completely through the box and protrude an additional 6 to 8 in. They should also be close enough to the neck (1½ to 2 in) so the strings are within easy reach of the index finger and thumb, the playing fingers.

3 Cut holes in box and insert the three wood components, see photograph on p 76.

4 Mark placement of zither pins on one side of the neck at approximately 1 in intervals starting about 2 in from the end. On the opposite side of the neck, pins will start at 2½ in from the end at 1 in intervals so that they will slightly offset and not bump into pins on the other side. Drill and attach zither pins to the neck.

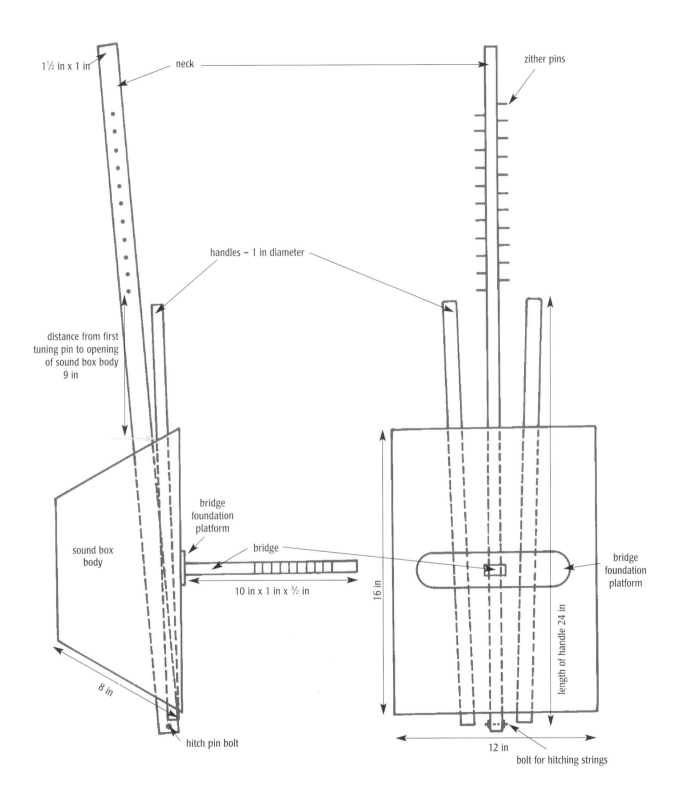

1½ in x 1 in

neck

zither pins

handles – 1 in diameter

distance from first
tuning pin to opening
of sound box body
9 in

bridge
foundation
platform

bridge

sound box
body

10 in x 1 in x ³⁄₂ in

16 in

bridge
foundation
platform

length of handle 24 in

8 in

hitch pin bolt

12 in

bolt for hitching strings

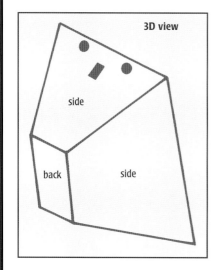

3D view

side

back   side

Placement of neck and handles to sound box.

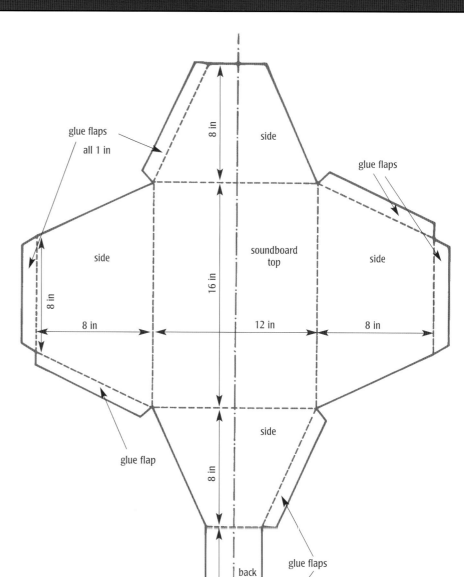

glue flaps
all 1 in

8 in   side

glue flaps

side   soundboard
top   side

16 in

8 in

8 in   12 in   8 in

glue flap

side

8 in

glue flaps

back

8 in

4 in

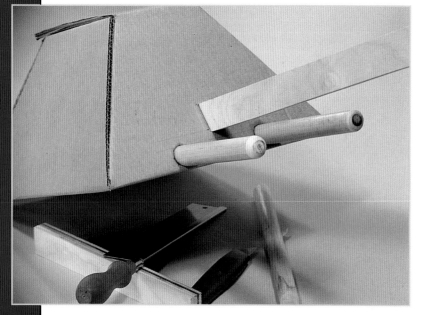

5 Make the vertical bridge from a 10 in scrap of the same material used for the neck. Saw shallow notches at ½ in increments along opposite edges of the bridge starting about 4½ in from the soundboard. Double check string trajectories with a long ruler making sure the shortest strings pass freely from neck to bridge without bumping into the box. Strings should be approximately ½ in apart through the playing area.
6 Strings will tie off at the tail end of the instrument. They should be well-anchored because this number of strings can exert a great deal of pulling power. Use a small bolt for this purpose.

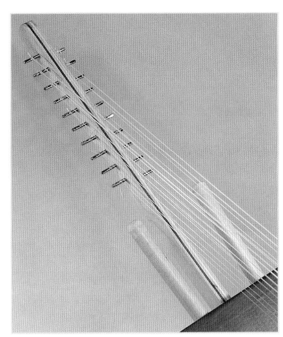

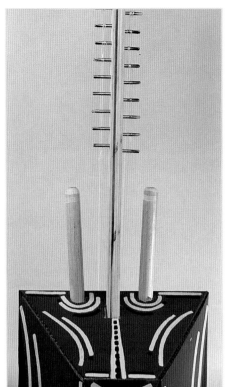

Above *Tuning pin arrangement*
Top right *View from the back of the kora*

7 Since the top of the box is vulnerable to the down-bearing pressure of the bridge, a wood foundation platform for the bridge is positioned and glued to the box to help protect the box and distribute the vibrations.

8 Attach nylon strings from tailpiece, through their respective bridge notches, and onto their respective zither pins. Secure for tuning. Depending on how many strings you decide to use, three or four gauges of string may be desirable to create a smooth sounding scale. Experiment and make adjustments, as necessary.

9 Tune opposing strings to the same pitch. This arrangement facilitates interesting rhythmic possibilities between the hands.

Left *Arrangement of strings on bridge*
Right *Kora strung and ready to play*

Greek Lyre

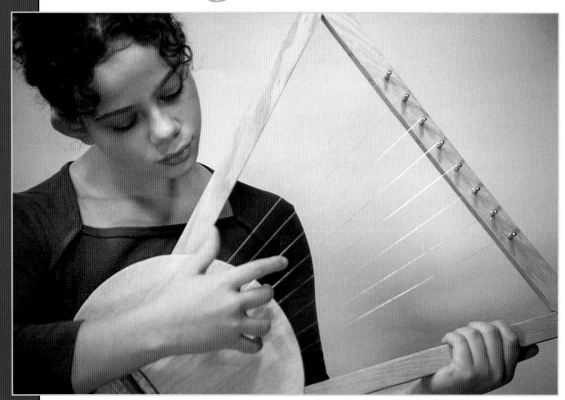

The lyre is characterized by its two-arm and crossbar construction. It was popular throughout the ancient world and retains a mystique even today.

Materials

a slice of large diameter
    cardboard tubing for
    sound box body
hardwood sticks for arms
    and crossbar
$\frac{1}{8}$ in plywood for
    soundboard and back
wood pieces for bridge
zither pins
hitch pins
music wire strings

Procedure

1 Cut a 4 in segment from a 10 in or larger diameter cardboard tube.

2 Using this tube sound box as a pattern, cut two pieces of $\frac{1}{8}$ in plywood for the top and back of the lyre. Set aside.

3 Cut hardwood stick into three pieces to conform to the traditional lyre configuration. Measurements used are 1 in x $\frac{3}{4}$ in x 24 in for the arms and 20 in for the crossbar.

4 Arrange the two arms so they converge at the tail-end of the instrument and mark their placement on the sound box as they pass out towards the crossbar.

5 Cut notches in the tubing so the arms fit snugly, as shown. Measure and cut the crossbar based on the resulting configuration.

6 Secure the entire framework using lap joints at the arm/crossbar junctions. Tack, glue, or screw. Where the arms converge inside the sound box, a simple butt joint, fitted and glued, will suffice (see photo p 79).

Above *Cutting out soundboard*
Right *Fitting arms to sound box*

7 Make a bridge/platform combination 3½ in x 1½ in x ¾ in which will help distribute the pressure and sound of the strings. Glue to soundboard.

8 Drill desired number of zither pin holes equidistant (approximately 1¼ in apart) along the crossbar and attach tuners. Drill and attach two or more sturdy hitch pins to the tail end for securing strings at that point.

9 Cut shallow grooves in bridge and position to keep strings lined up.

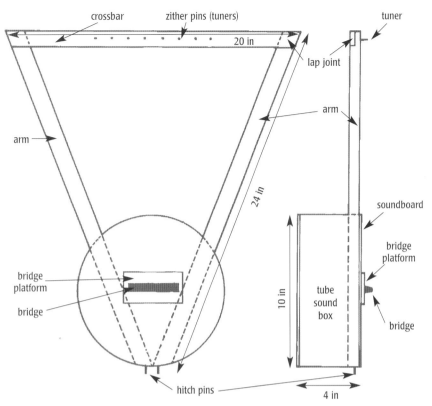

10 Attach and tension strings to desired pitches. A common diatonic scale is a good place to start. Minor modes sound particularly attractive when played on the lyre.

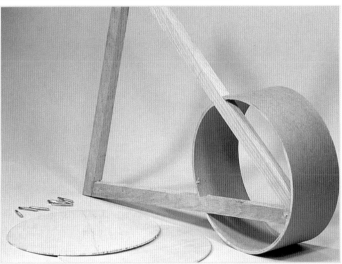

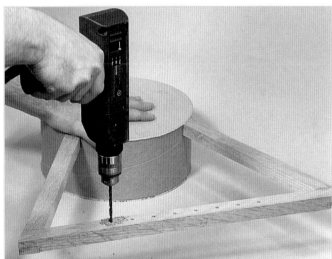

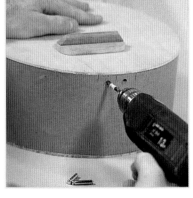

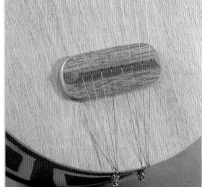

Top *Lap joint at arm crossbar junction*
Above left *Ready to glue top and back*
Above right *Drill zither pin holes along crossbar*
Bottom left *Drill for hitch pins*
Bottom right *Bridge arrangement*

Index